YOUR PERSONAL FINANCIAL FITNESS PROGRAM

1987–88 Edition

YOUR PERSONAL FINANCIAL FITNESS PROGRAM

1987–88 Edition

Elizabeth S. Lewin, CFP

Facts On File Publications
New York, New York ● Oxford, England

Your Personal Financial Fitness Program
1987–88 Edition

Library of Congress Cataloging-in-Publication Data

Lewin, Elizabeth.
    Your personal financial fitness program.

    Includes index.
    1. Finance, Personal. I. Title.
HG179.L48 1987   332.024   86-29093
ISBN 0-8160-1580-5

Printed in U.S.A.
10 9 8 7 6 5 4 3 2 1

"Thinking about money is an activity which can send one into a state that borders on anything from a slight uneasiness to terror."
from Bread Upon the Waters by
Irwin Shaw
Delacorte Press

ACKNOWLEDGMENTS

This book would not have been possible without the assistance of Bernard Ryan Jr. I also wish to thank Muriel Greenblatt, Consultant for Community Relations, Center 60, Chase Manhattan Bank; Anita Greenhut; Martha Hirsch, Nexus Center, Hamden, CT.; Laventhol & Horwath, Certified Public Accountants; Celine M. Lynam, Benefits Manager, Moore McCormack Resources; Harold Schifreen, CFP, Herzfeld, Stern, Inc.; TRW; Hamilton Wilson, Gonsor, Wilson Communications, Westport, CT.; and Pauline Wilson, American Women's Economic Development.

To Loraine Grover Wallace whose need gave me the idea for the book. To Mike Dworken, Certified Public Accountant who lent ideas and support to the project. And to my children Valerie and Eric.

CONTENTS

WHY I WROTE THIS BOOK FOR YOU

If you have ever made the discovery that money doesn't stretch as far as you expect it to...if you have ever hoped or prayed for a way to eliminate the frustration that arises from financial turmoil...this book is for you.

It is for singles, for couples starting out in marriage and couples in mid-stream with large or small families, for the widowed, the divorced and the retired—and especially for those who are in transition from one such stage to another. It is for anyone who needs practical, instructive ways to control his or her own finances.

My Total Financial Fitness Program grew out of the many seminars I have given. Their purpose is to build confidence and create a sense of security about handling money in much the same way a physical fitness program builds confidence and security about your weight, muscle tone and health. When your body is out of shape, you know you need a physical fitness program. When handling money gets out of control, you need this Financial Fitness Program.

That's why I wrote this book—to help you meet that need. And to help you see that even if you are in a crunch, you don't need a lot of money to get out of it.

I urge you to use this book in a very direct way. Study the sample worksheets. Get acquainted with the three typical families (one from each of three generations) that show you how financial situations are linked directly to life situations. Then start filling out your own individual worksheets. Use a pencil with a good eraser, and don't be afraid to use the eraser end, too! Feel free to photocopy the worksheets for your personal use.

Above all, take your time. Like a physical fitness program, my Total Financial Fitness Program cannot be done in one sitting. If you try to cram it all together, you will gain frustrations—not control.

Finally—and also like physical fitness—remember that the more you work and gain control, the better you will feel and the more fun you will have.

Elizabeth Lewin

YOUR PERSONAL FINANCIAL FITNESS PROGRAM

How to Manage Your Own Money in a Few Minutes a Day

WHY MANAGE MONEY?

1

"How come my money runs out before the month runs out?"
"There's another call from somebody who wants to get paid!"
"Oh, dear—where did I put that insurance policy?"

Sooner or later, almost everyone gets in a quandary over money matters. Most people feel they need help, but they don't always know where to begin. When people come to my Personal Financial Fitness seminars, they are usually surprised to discover that they don't have to drown in a flood of papers, or stew about unpaid bills, or feel embarrassed because they can't seem to manage.

It is my job to help people understand their money needs, and to help them realize that they have feelings about money—just as they have feelings about every other subject that is vital to them. These feelings are an integral part of their attitudes and abili-

ties where handling money is concerned. At the same time, it is my job to help them become financially fit by learning to manage their money—both for the immediate future and for the years ahead.

The goal: control your money

The only way to be financially fit is to get control of your own finances. That is the purpose of this book—to help *you* get control of your money. Just like a physical fitness program, it requires some exercises. But instead of calisthenics, you'll be doing your exercises with a pencil. If you keep on the program, you'll be as financially fit as anyone could desire.

If you are confused, or think you are confused, about money, you are certainly not alone. There is plenty to get confused about, from continuing changes in tax laws, inflation, fluctuations in interest rates, and new ways to invest, to the buy-now pay-later world of the credit card.

You may feel standoffish or inadequate when it comes to money matters. Most people do. Most people don't even like to think about money and are afraid to look at their own situation. It is always out of control, they feel. Their incomes are too small for long-range planning or even for immediate planning. Besides, planning takes too much time. How could it be worth it?

That is the key to Financial Fitness. Planning *is* worth it. No matter how large or small your income, planning can put you fully in charge of it. Planning can make you the boss of your financial destiny. And you do not have to be a financial wizard to plan how to handle your money and make educated decisions.

Planning answers the "what ifs"

Planning can get you ready to answer the "what if" questions that are so important in life:

"What if I buy a new car now?"
"What if I take out another loan—can my lifestyle stand it?"
"What if we sell the house now?"
"What if we have our first baby this year?"
"What if I lost my job?"

All of the "what if" questions (and you may be able to think of dozens more) fall into one of the five main categories of financial planning:

1   Coping with an emergency
2   Saving for future expenses
3   Maintaining adequate insurance
4   Providing the income for retirement
5   Preserving and maximizing an estate for survivors.

Planning is also important to your emotional security. With financial planning under control, you reduce risks, avoid anxiety over spending, and manage to increase savings. You are ready to cope with unexpected and unplanned expenses that can adversely affect your resources, such as a relocation, a divorce, the death of a spouse or a parent, disability, loss of a job, even the arrival of a child.

While many people hope and wish that nothing would ever change, life is change and change affects finances. Let's look at just three major changes that affect most people:

1.   *Living alone.* More than 80 percent of today's women will live alone during some period of their lives, probably because of divorce or widowhood. Many divorced women must exist on less money than they have become accustomed to. And many find themselves having to manage money for the first time. Simply learning to balance the checkbook, let alone planning several years of higher education for their children, can be traumatic for women with no financial experience. Widows often feel intellectually ill-equipped to handle their own money and make financial decisions, even in situations where retirement and estate planning have been carefully considered beforehand.

2.   *Debt.* Consumer debt is now over $300 billion. Many couples have kept up with the Joneses via a spending spree three decades long—and find themselves bogged deeply in debt. Today's income no longer covers yesterday's excesses and a terrible double drain occurs: While a large proportion of income must be paid out to reduce debt, inflation raises the cost of basic expenses. The result? Some people borrow to cover basic living expenses—a near-suicidal lifestyle.

3.   *Retirement.* The retirement years are supposed to be sun-filled, but those near retirement age can no longer look ahead confidently to a comfortable condominium in Florida or Arizona. Sadly, inflation has made the traditional retirement income from Social Security and pensions inadequate for most people. Many are now reevaluating their assets and studying alternative ways to make the money they have saved contribute to total income.

You will be surprised how much frustration can be eliminated from your life by becoming and staying financially fit. And you will be especially thankful when a crisis or major change occurs, as one inevitably will, and you find that you have come through it with financial matters under control.

Only you can do it

One other point: Like physical exercise, no one can do it for you. You cannot leave money matters to fate, for fate can be cruel. You cannot leave them until some future time, for they will not go away. And you cannot, over the long haul, leave them to someone else, for ultimately management of your money will become your business and yours alone. Leaving financial matters to fate, the future, or others will simply create more problems for you.

Once you've gotten used to managing your money, though, you can relax. Financial Fitness will become part of day-to-day living, as much a part of your routine as shopping for groceries or getting the laundry done.

No one plans to fail. But most of us fail to plan. The first and most essential step in planning is to get your thinking and your record-keeping organized. One will increase the effectiveness of the other.

The next two chapters deal with these aspects of Financial Fitness: thinking about where you want to go and the kind of record-keeping that will help you decide whether you are on the right road.

INTRODUCING THREE VERY SPECIAL FAMILIES . . .

Say hello to three generations of one family: the Youngs, the Mids, and the Elders. Each is a typical family of today who will turn up now and then in these pages to illustrate how some of the principles and advice in this book can be used to apply to those who are just starting out, those who have well-established homes and families, and those who have reached retirement age.

Dolly and James Young

The Youngs have been married for four years. They are now in their mid-twenties and have a baby a little over a year old.

The Youngs met in college and were married soon after graduation. Jim went to work for the Madison Ice Cream Company at an annual salary of $19,000. Dolly, working full-time as a teacher, started at $14,000, so their combined gross income before taxes was $33,000. Jim then went to night school to earn his master's in business administration.

The Youngs rented a one-bedroom apartment. Their immediate goal was to furnish the apartment and save for a house or condominium. Along with the furnishings came a stereo, and a new car for Dolly—plus a new kind of lifestyle in order to keep up with their friends. This included eating out a great deal, which was much more convenient with both of them working.

When Dolly became pregnant two years later (an event that was not planned), the Youngs decided to move into a two-bedroom apartment. They bought more furnishings, adding to their existing charge account at the furniture store. To keep up their lifestyle, Dolly returned to work part-time after the baby was born—this time as a secretary, not a teacher. Luckily, she was able to work out a joint baby-sitting service with another young mother who lived nearby.

Up to now, with little or no cash on hand, the Youngs have been using charge cards to buy almost everything they need. They realize that before they can plan a second child they must get their act together, get themselves out of debt, and start a savings program so they can buy the house they want. They intend to "bare-bone" it for the next year or so.

Currently Jim Young earns $27,500 and Dolly, working half-time, is bringing in $7,500, so their combined gross income—one child later—is $35,000 or $2,000 more than when they started.

Jim Young gets good fringe benefits at the Madison Ice Cream Company, including Blue Cross, major medical, a dental plan, and a group life insurance policy that provides coverage of $30,000. He is enrolled in the company pension plan but is not yet vested.

The Youngs' situation is this: They have acquired a great many consumer goods, but they have almost nothing in assets. Since they are spending everything they both bring home, they have no resources or emergency funds. In any sort of crisis, the assets they have in material goods will produce no income or other assistance.

Mary and Marty Mid

Marty was born in 1935, Mary a couple of years later. Children of the World War II years, they came along too late to be aware of how tight things had been financially during the Great Depression.

Marty does remember the long hours his mother worked on the night shift in the local men's suit factory, which had converted to making army uniforms, and his father's worry in the late years of the war over whether he would be drafted from his job processing photographic chemicals. (Because he had two children and was doing needed war work, he was not drafted.) And Marty remembers how his parents talked of whether the end of the war would reduce their earning power (both were getting top overtime pay). Always his mother would stress his getting a college education so he would never be laid off by the kind of bad times his parents remembered.

Marty started college just toward the end of the Korean War, went into the army after his freshman year, and afterward was able to go back to college and finish under the G.I. bill.

Mary had been his high school sweetheart, and they were married at the end of his sophomore year in college. She worked as a secretary during his last two years of college and before their first child, a daughter, was born in 1961.

After he graduated, Marty worked for a series of firms. Then in 1965 he joined the accounting department of the company where he works today. The Mids lived first in apartments. In the late 1960s, after their third child was born, they bought their first home. They sold it in 1973 to buy their present, $50,000 house.

The Mids' goal when they were first married was to buy their own home. When their daughter was born, Mary stayed home to raise her, and she remained at home while the next two were little. The Mids' long-term goal was to save substantially, especially for their children's educations—a top priority.

Marty's salary increased steadily and the Mids managed to live comfortably, to take family vacations, to furnish their home as they wanted. They used credit only for car payments and an occasional home improvement loan; otherwise they waited until they could afford any major purchase, for they wanted to avoid being caught as their parents had been.

As the children approached college age, however, the Mids realized that they could not pay for their education just with their savings and the income from one salary. So Mary went back to work as a part-time secretary. Her income is devoted to helping to pay college costs.

Gertrude and Frank Elder

The Elders came to America as children, with their parents. Frank went to technical school and became a skilled mechanic. Gertrude worked in a factory. They married in 1933, and during the Depression one of them was usually working. They had one child and lived in half of a two-family house on a quiet side street.

World War II found Frank Elder still young enough to serve, but his skills as a mechanic kept him deferred from the military. He worked long overtime hours, earning good money that he and his wife were able to save.

Gertrude did volunteer work during the war. Afterward she stayed home as a housewife and the Elders put their savings into a new home. Both worked steadily at landscaping and improving their property.

Until he retired at 65, Frank Elder was always employed. However, he worked at a number of different places and never had the benefit of a pension plan—a fact that did not bother the Elders for Frank was always saving for their retirement. As their nest egg grew, the Elders invested in America's future by buying "blue chip" stocks. They lived simply. They saved. They invested. They were ready if ever another Depression came along.

Sometimes the Elders took carefully budgeted vacations. One such trip found them in the sunny Southwest. Deciding they liked the steady warm climate, they bought a small lot.

When they retired in 1977, Frank and Gertrude sold their home for $30,000. They bought a new car and paid cash, so as not to incur any debt at this time. It had all the extras that would allow them to travel comfortably to the Southwest. They put a prefabricated house on their lot, and added drapes and carpeting and some new furniture. After moving expenses were paid, they had $7,500 in cash left over.

Things have not gone as expected for the Elders. Frank gets $714.00 a month from Social Security. This includes all benefit increases that have occurred since he retired. Since Gertrude started taking Social Security benefits at age 62, she gets $268 a month. If she had waited until she was 65, she would be getting $357.

Expenses have soared since the Elders moved to the Southwest. Electricity and water are way up; in fact, utility costs have quadrupled. Gasoline has skyrocketed. Since they bought a lot far out of town, purposely to get away from the kind of built-up neighborhood they were used to, the Elders use the car a great deal. It now has high mileage and needs frequent repair.

Many of the auto trips to town are for medical care: a seemingly never-ending saga that includes unreimbursed office visits, new glasses, drugs, dental work, an operation, and another illness. "The bills are killing us," says Frank. "We keep shelling out for insurance but it doesn't pick up so many of the bills. We're living from hand to mouth."

The Elders had planned to travel the Southwest, to dine out frequently, to get back East now and then to see family and old friends. Instead, they rely on the telephone for the visits back home, but make sure to keep an eye on the phone bill. They find that despite the cost the telephone helps them to feel less isolated from the family.

Frank Elder sums it up: "We sit here among the other angry senior citizens, spending our savings for necessities—not for fun."

SETTING YOUR FINANCIAL FITNESS GOALS

2

Even if a chorus of Annies belt out "Tomorrow! Tomorrow! Tomorrow!" most of us don't like to face up to the needs of the future. Education for the kids? A new house? Retirement and travel? Who knows?

Only *you* know. And only you can put your goals on paper and so design your Financial Fitness Program to reach them.

Realistic financial goals do several things:

- They establish a framework for financial stability.
- They help you to utilize your income to best advantage.
- They help you to accept the reality of your particular situation so you can learn not to spend against a dream.

How do you establish your own goals?

Start by asking yourself, "What's important to me?" Your goals reflect your value system—usually the attitudes you were raised with. For most of us, values are based on what is desirable and worthy. And, for most of us, value systems aren't usually very flexible. If you're old enough to be working with this book, chances are your attitudes have been pretty much set for quite some time now.

Within the framework of goals, based on your values and attitudes, you'll have priorities—goals that are most important.

Values dictate behavior

Now comes the catch: How do you actually behave when it comes to finances? If your behavior is not consistent with your values, attitudes, and goals, you are off base.

Say you've been raised with a value system which holds that education is of prime importance: College is therefore a must for your children, a goal that may dictate saving $100 a month. But say your behavior is not consistent with your goal. You decide you cannot afford to save $100 a month for education, or you put some other goal first. Your behavior shows that your goal of college for your children is of lower priority.

Most people need to establish priorities among their financial goals because their desires often exceed their resources.

Take a good hard look at your goals and your behavior. Is your behavior helping you to achieve your goals, or hindering you?

Conflict: A couple or an individual may have two goals which cannot both be satisfied because achieving one prevents achieving the other.

Short, Mid & Long-Range Goals

A *short-range goal* is something you want to do next year. Pay off a loan, say. Or plan Christmas shopping money in advance, instead of paying off bills through winter and spring. Or buy a vacation in advance, so you can really enjoy it, instead of moaning as the VISA and Mastercard charges mount up.

A *middle-range goal* is something you want to do in, say, three to five years. Buy a second home, perhaps, or a better car, or take a trip abroad. Maybe you want to plan on having another child (yes, at today's projected costs of approximately $200,000 from age 0 to 21, a child is a middle-range goal).

A *long-range goal* covers such items as education and retirement.

Agreement on goals

Goals have another dimension besides time: family commitment. Certainly you and your wife or husband must talk freely, openly, and at length about goals. But also include your children in discussions. If you and your spouse and your children communicate your individual financial objectives and reach an understanding about them, you can all avoid many arguments and financial crises. Many, many misunderstandings about money develop simply because people haven't let their goals be known.

Remember that the primary objective of a viable plan is the accumulation of money, or capital.

Everything else in your financial plan is directed to achieving this goal.

Thus you must not only define your goals but follow through on the details. If your children's education is a top goal, take the time now to estimate what it will cost. Use today's dollars, then update the figure once a year, just as you update the grocery budget to meet inflation.

What you are trying to avoid, of course, is waking up one day to find that you have to borrow to meet a goal such as education.

Goals and needs keep changing. They should be checked every year. Never feel that you must stay locked into a specific goal. But, by the same token, never use the money set aside for a medium or long-term goal to pay for something you want now.

Important: List your goals. Give each one a dollar amount and a time frame.

MARY AND MARTY MID HAVE THREE BASIC GOALS . . .

First, they want to be sure they provide the last important year of education for their daughter. This is their immediate *short-range* goal.

Second is their *mid-range* goal: to give themselves the long touring vacation they have put off for a number of years while educating their children.

Third is their *long-range* goal: to plan a retirement that maintains the lifestyle they are accustomed to. This is a major concern, as they realize that the Elders are not having the kind of retirement they expected.

Setting goals accomplishes several things. It forces you and your family to examine your values and clarify them. It enables you to devise ways to use your available resources to attain your goals. And it puts you in charge, makes you take control of your life and your money.

On the next page you will find the first Financial Fitness worksheet. Each time you come to a worksheet you'll find at least one completed as an example and a blank one for you to fill out. The first worksheet is **Saving for a Specific Goal**. Let's look

Worksheet I: Example
Mr. & Mrs. Mid
SAVING FOR A SPECIFIC GOAL

A. GOAL _____ RETIREMENT _____

B. DATE NEEDED _____ 12/3/01 _____

C. NUMBER OF YEARS TILL GOAL _____ 14 _____

D. AMOUNT NEEDED _____ $200,000 _____

E. MONEY ALREADY SET ASIDE _____ NONE _____

F. AMOUNT MONEY SET ASIDE WILL
GROW TO AT _____ % _____ — _____

G. AMOUNT STILL NEEDED _____ $200,000 _____

H. AMOUNT TO BE SAVED PER YEAR
AT ___10___ % INTEREST _____ $7,150 _____

together at how the Mids have filled it out (see above). They have established the goal as their retirement. To maintain the lifestyle they are accustomed to, they will want to have spendable income of $25,000 after taxes. But by the year 2001 (if we assume that a five percent annual rate of inflation will continue), they will need double that—or about $50,000 after taxes—in their first year of retirement. So they must accumulate about $200,000 to meet that goal. The figure in line H is the amount that they have to save each year, assuming a 10 percent interest. This figure comes from the Financial Compound Interest and Annuity Tables. Check with your bank, insurance agent or accountant who has ready access to this particular book. Now, decide what your saving goal is and fill out the worksheet on page 10.

Whatever your age, establishing your own goals should also make you aware of the goals of others who are younger or older. Goals for the recently married are quite different from those of their parents or grandparents. Most young couples don't need two cars. Most parents of teenage children—or of schoolchildren of any age, in many cases—need a second car. A retired couple usually needs but one car.

Keep your behavior in mind, and under control. Your Financial Fitness Program must be compatible and consistent with your goals—otherwise you're headed for conflict and trouble.

Worksheet I: Yours
SAVING FOR A SPECIFIC GOAL

A. GOAL

B. DATE NEEDED

C. NUMBER OF YEARS TILL GOAL

D. AMOUNT NEEDED

E. MONEY ALREADY SET ASIDE

F. AMOUNT MONEY SET ASIDE WILL
GROW TO AT _____ %

G. AMOUNT STILL NEEDED

H. AMOUNT TO BE SAVED PER YEAR
AT _____ % INTEREST

THE FOUNDATION OF FINANCIAL FITNESS: YOUR RECORD SYSTEM

3

Every night at 10 P.M. a New York television station asks its audience, "Do you know where your children are?": a sensible reminder of parental responsibility.

The station would be performing another valuable public service if it occasionally asked, "Do you know where your life insurance policies are?" or "Do you know where the certificate of title to your automobile is?"

A good record-keeping system is an important part of Financial Fitness. Financial Fitness means being able to prove what you spent, where you spent it, what you spent it for, and how it improved or failed to improve your financial situation. What you need for all this is *records*: not a mountain of paper but a practical system for keeping track of financial matters, and important papers related to them, over a long period of time.

You should begin keeping records from your first job on through retirement. The record-keeping itself can be a simple file system of various papers, some

items being permanent, some semi-permanent, others temporary. For instance, obviously you keep a life insurance policy as long as it is in force. You keep automobile papers as long as you own the car. You keep home improvement receipts until you sell the house and want to prove how much extra capital you have put into it over the years. You keep ordinary sales receipts and other income tax records for three years, until the statute of limitations runs out: An audit by the Internal Revenue Service (IRS) may go back no more than three years. However, you should keep your final IRS tax return for each year in a permanent file. It makes an excellent financial history.

A costly failing

Not having a good system of record-keeping can be not only embarrassing but costly. The newly widowed woman who cannot find her husband's life insurance policies suffers embarrassment as well as grief. The widow who has a very good offer for her husband's classic automobile but cannot find the certificate of title may wait weeks for the molasses-like motor vehicle department to issue a new one—and thus lose the sale. The difference between the first offer and the next to come along may be $500 or more. The widow who was never told by her ex-GI husband that he had a paid-up service insurance policy put away somewhere goes without the proceeds for which she is eligible.

You don't have to be newly widowed to lose money in another way. Banks regularly take out local newspaper advertisements to list the names and last known addresses of thousands of customers who have left accounts inactive for a specified period of time.

The fact is that billions of dollars from bank accounts are held in state treasuries simply because no one can trace the assets to their rightful owners. If a bank account is totally inactive for a certain number of years (the period varies from state to state), and if the bank fails to locate the owner after placing an advertisement listing the last known address, the unclaimed money goes to the state.

By the same token, if you own a piece of property, move away, forget to tell the tax assessor where you have gone and then fail to pay the taxes (every year it is astonishing how many people can and do forget such things), the town may auction that parcel of land to the highest bidder—and keep the proceeds.

Some states exact a personal property tax on cars and boats. In this computer age, any motor vehicle department can make a quick check on whether tax has been paid on an automobile and will refuse to renew a car's registration if it has not. One of my clients sold his boat and did not save the bill of sale. Months later the state demanded tax due on the boat. To prove the boat had been sold and he owed no tax, my client had to trace the boat dealer to Florida and get another receipt.

Ever try to reconstruct the history of an illness a year or more after you got well? Many have—all because they didn't make medical records promptly and hang onto them. With most doctors' offices asking for payment at the time of your visit and

---

Exhibit 1
UNCLAIMED BANK ACCOUNT NOTICE

RE: 1031520,   Balance 167.24

Dear Customers:

   According to our records, we have a Savings Account in your name which has been inactive for more than 10 years. State Laws regarding abandoned property require banks to remit the balance of accounts 10 years or more inactive to the Treasurer of the State of Connecticut.

   In order to activate your account, please mail or present your passbook to us to be updated. Please notify us if your passbook has been lost. Enclosed is a bank by mail envelope for your convenience.

   If we do not hear from you within ten days from receipt of this letter, the account will automatically be remitted to the State of Connecticut.

Very truly yours,

Enc.

leaving it up to you to handle major medical and other insurance claims, it is important to make a habit of getting a photocopy of all receipts and claim forms and of filing all claims promptly.

If your doctor (or hospital or lab) was not paid at the time of your visit and you are reimbursed by an insurance company, it is important that you immediately pay the bill rather than spend the money and say, "Oh, I'll take care of the doctor [or hospital or lab] later."

Many records can be replaced, but it takes time, effort and postage to replace them. Take stock certificates. If you own more than one or two, you should have an accurate list by name, number of shares, purchase price, and date of purchase. Compiling such a list after your certificates have been lost, stolen, or destroyed can be a horrendous task, and the result may be incomplete. Before any company will issue a replacement certificate, you will have to sign an affidavit that the certificate was destroyed and put up a surety bond, which can cost as much as 3 percent of the current market price.

What goes to the bank, what stays home

Where should you keep important papers and records? You should keep some in a safe deposit box in a bank, and others at home in a safe and sensible file.

Best kept in a safe deposit box are those papers that are difficult to replace, including:

Birth certificates
Stock certificates
Marriage certificate
Citizenship papers
Bonds
Certificate of title for an automobile
Real estate deeds
Copy of will (but not the original)
Divorce decree
Death certificates
Passports
Discharge from military service
Veterans Administration papers
Adoption papers
Contracts
Household inventory (with photographs for appraisal purposes)

Why don't life insurance policies and the original copy of your will go into the safe deposit box? Because in most states when the owner, or joint owner, of a safe deposit box dies, the bank seals the box until all tax and legal matters are taken care of. Access is granted only when the bank receives legal permission, and then in the presence of an authorized person. A life insurance company will not pay a claim until the policy is surrendered. The probation of a will cannot begin until the last will is presented to the probate court. Thus, everything is held up if legal permission to open a safe deposit box must be obtained.

The best place to keep your life insurance policies is at home. The best place to keep your will is in the files of the attorney who drew it up.

After reading the examples for Mr. and Mrs. Mid, fill out the worksheets at the end of this chapter on **Personal Information** (II), **Personal Contacts** (III), **Record Keeping** (IV), and **Location of Other Important Papers** (V). Detail is important; better to jot down too much than too little.

Some of these details may seem obvious. Some may look like a nuisance to get hold of. Just remember they will not seem obvious to anyone who must track down all this information if you're not around to supply it. And lawyers can tell you how much they are paid to take care of "nuisance" details you could easily have had ready in a file.

When you have filled out these sheets, get duplicates made. Give a set to someone else to keep for you, someone who will understand the method of your madness.

File—and throw out

Your filing system? It can be an elaborate, decorated file cabinet or a collection of shoe boxes. What counts is not what it looks like but how well you have organized it. The key is to get into the habit of filing those papers that are important and *throwing out* those that are not.

Your permanent home file should include:

Annuities
Automobile insurance
Bankbooks and statements
Children's records
Credit histories

Disability insurance policy
Educational records (for each member of family)
Employment history
Federal income tax returns
Gift tax returns
Gifts
Health insurance coverage and policies
Health records
Home improvements
Homeowner's insurance
Household inventory (with receipts and appraisals)
Inheritances
Insurance policies (if not filed under subject headings, such as auto, medical, and so on)
IRA (individual retirement account)
Keogh plan
Life insurance policies
List of important advisors
Loan applications
Loans
Medical insurance
Medicare
Money market funds
Mutual funds
Paid bills
Pension and profit-sharing plans
Property tax bills and receipts
Real estate investments
Social Security earnings records
Social Security numbers
State income tax returns
Stock options
Stock and bond record book
Warranties and guarantees
Wills (file signed original with attorney)

A word about records of stock and bond transactions and home improvements. This is strictly a matter of keeping good records for tax purposes.

If you use a stock and bond record book, use a different colored pen for each year in which you have stock transactions. If you are using blue ink for this year, for instance, you will know that all blue ink items that are sold must be included in this year's tax return.

It is important to have a record of when you bought a particular stock, and at what price. When you sell it, it will be necessary to figure out the gain or loss on the sale. Many years may have passed between the purchase and the sale, and you will have to pay a tax on the profit.

The same is true of your house or condominium. When you sell, you will pay a tax on the profit (that is, the difference between the original purchase price and the sale price). But every permanent improvement made over the years may be deducted from the profit: landscaping, for instance, or converting a garage to a playroom, installing insulation and other energy-saving devices, the addition of a building, swimming pool, deck, or patio, or doing anything else that added value to the house. An accurate record of bills paid and canceled checks will be invaluable when the house is sold.

Before moving out, take pictures in and around the house. When you prepare your tax return, they will help jog your memory. You'll be surprised at how many deductible improvements you will see in these photographs.

SUPPOSE MR. AND MRS. MID DECIDE TO SELL THEIR HOUSE...

They find that with appreciation over the years since they bought it in 1973 (mostly due to inflation), their split level purchased for $50,000 can now be sold for over $100,000. If they sell it for $100,000 before they are 55 years old, they must pay a capital gains tax on $50,000 of the price. (Those over 55 benefit from a once-in-a-lifetime exemption of $125,000 when selling a house.) But the Mids' well-kept records can cut down the tax bite:

House purchased 1973		$50,000
Permanent improvements:		
landscaping	$3,000	
insulation	1,000	
carpeting	1,500	
garage converted to playroom	8,000	
new driveway	2,000	
	$15,500	$15,500
		$65,500

Selling price	$100,000
Less costs of improvements and original purchase price	65,500
Capital gains tax is calculated on	$ 34,500

For your annual income tax return, a continuing file is vital. If the IRS decides to audit your return, the burden of proof will be on you. By the same token, an accordian file of canceled checks, organized by categories, will help you with budget planning as well as tax returns. Categories include such items as:

Automobile expenses
Bills from specific stores
Children's expenses
Clothing
Contributions
Education
Entertainment and recreation
Household expenses (maintenance)
Household purchases (major)
Insurance premiums
Medical and dental expenses
Mortgage payments
Taxes (real estate and personal property)
Utilities

With this file at your fingertips, you can tackle a new year's budgeting and your end-of-year tax return with confidence in your accuracy. Many bills can then be thrown out (yes, this is worth repeating, because it is so hard to get people to realize that "throw out" means what it says). Only those bills needed as evidence for tax purposes need be saved.

If the IRS audits you

A cardinal rule: Always remember that the IRS does not understand the words "I can't find it." If you want to prove something, such as an expenditure, you must show up with the proof in your hand.

In fact, the IRS considers you guilty until you prove yourself innocent. It is permitted by law to audit you for three years from the date you file a return. For example, if your 1980 return was filed on April 15, 1981, you may be audited on it at any time until April 15, 1984, but no later. (Exception: The IRS is legally entitled to audit you at a later date if it expects to charge you with fraud or gross negligence.) Once the three years have passed, you should *throw out* most of your canceled checks and documentation, keeping only those items that have to do with possible future capital gains tax information, such as home improvements or purchase of collectibles and stocks and bonds.

A word about IRS audits. Being called in for an audit evokes horror in most people's minds, equivalent to the feeling produced by the words "root canal" at the dentist's. What can you do?

Be prepared is the answer. Your notice from the IRS will indicate the sections of your tax return that it wants to check on. The letter will tell you to call for an appointment, probably at the nearest IRS office. If your return was prepared by an accountant, contact him or her and see if the accountant will go in your place; it's best to check if there will be an additional fee for this service. If you decide to make an appearance yourself, take with you all the bills and canceled checks relating to the particular items the IRS has said it wants to check on.

Important: Keep your eyes and ears open and your mouth closed as much as possible in an IRS meeting. Answer only the questions you are asked. Do not chitchat. Control the natural tendency to babble in nervous situations. Concentrate on counting the holes in the ceiling tiles, if you must, but fight the urge to blurt out something you may regret. Let out your primal scream when you get out of the office.

There are indeed emotional aspects to recordkeeping. Being able to put your hands on the right piece of paper, at the moment you need it, is the greatest relief ever devised for an anxiety attack. If you have taken the precaution of letting someone else in on the secret of your method, you will be in much better shape during an unexpected period of transition or emotional turmoil.

Worksheet II: Example
Mr. & Mrs. Mid
RECORD-KEEPING
Personal Information

Yourself:

1. Name __Martin Mid__ Address __846 Tower Ct.__
   City/State __Iowa City, Iowa 52240__ Telephone Number __(319) 555-1212__
   Place of Birth __Chicago, Ill.__ Date of Birth __12/03/35__
   Social Security # __987-65-4320__ Marital Status __Married__

2. Spouse's Name __Jane Elder Mid__ Address __846 Tower Ct.__
   City/State __Iowa City, Iowa 52240__ Telephone # __(319) 555-1212__
   Place of Birth __Chicago, Ill.__ Date of Birth __2/11/38__
   Social Security # __045-30-5867__

3. Children:

	1	2	3	4
Name	Dolly Young	John Mid	Sally Mid	
Address	1482 North St.	800 Park St.	College Dorm University of Michigan	
City/State	Denver, Colo.	Boston, Mass.	Ann Arbor, Mich.	
Telephone	(303) 823-3671	(617) 275-5600	(313) 996-8800	
Place of Birth	Chicago, Ill.	Iowa City	Iowa City	
Date of Birth	5/5/61	4/25/63	3/15/67	
Social Security #	042-68-1505	999-41-3841	868-11-9876	
Marital Status	Married	Single	Single	

4. Parents
   Name __deceased__ Address _____
   City/State _____ Telephone # _____
   Place of Birth _____ Date of Birth _____
   Mother's maiden name _____

5. Spouse's Parents
   Names __Gertrude & Frank Elder__ Address __41 Sun Drive__
   City/State __Desert City, Arizona__ Telephone __(602) 555-4615__
   Place of Birth __Mother Hungary / Father Germany__ Date of Birth __Mother 6/15/10 / Father 8/20/12__
   Mother's Maiden Name __Gosborg__

   Next of Kin:
   Name __James Mid__ Relationship __brother__
   Address __Peach Dr. Atlanta, Ga.__ Telephone # __(404) 525-3054__

   Neighbor or Close Friend
   Name __Elaine & John Wilson__ Address __2100 Tower Ct.__
   City/State __Iowa City, Iowa 52240__ Telephone __(319) 555-1000__

YOUR PERSONAL FINANCIAL FITNESS PROGRAM

Worksheet III: Example
Mr. & Mrs. Mid
RECORD-KEEPING
Personal Contacts

	NAME	ADDRESS	TELEPHONE NUMBER
Attorney	J. P. Brown	State Bank Building	(319) 555-6157
Accountant	P. W. Smith	State Bank Building	(319) 555-4100
Clergyman	Rev. Ray Ernest	First Church	(319) 555-6600
Stockbroker	None		
Physician	Dr. J. Green	University Hospital	(319) 555-7000
Trust Officer	None		
Banker	Ms. Mary Jones	State Bank	(319) 555-1234
Life Insurance Agent	John L. Long	83 Madison St.	(319) 555-4111
Other Insurance Agents			
Homeowner	Helen Blank	M. Horn & Co.	(319) 555-1111
Automobile	Helen Blank	M. Horn & Co.	(319) 555-1111
Medical	at work		
Disability	at work		
Executor of Estate	James Young		(303) 623-3671
Financial Planner	Elizabeth Lewin, CFP	Main St. Chicago, Ill.	(312) 930-7000
Others			

Worksheet IV: Example
Mr. & Mrs. Mid
RECORD-KEEPING

1. CHECKING ACCOUNTS, SAVINGS ACCOUNTS, CREDIT UNION ACCOUNTS, OTHER CASH ACCOUNTS

Name of Institution	Type and # of Account	Interest Rate	Current Balance	Owned By	Location of Checkbook or Passbooks
State Bank	checking 25098	0	$2,000	joint	pocket book
State Bank	money mkt. acc't 784432	varies	$20,000	joint	desk file

2. MONEY MARKET FUNDS, CERTIFICATES OF DEPOSIT, TREASURY BILLS AND NOTES

Name of Institution	Type and # of Account	Maturity Date	Amount Invested	Interest Rate	Owned by	Location of Passbooks

TOTAL

3. SECURITIES
Stocks & Mutual Funds:

Number of Shares	Company	Date Purchased	Total Cost	Current Market Value	Owned By	Location of Stock Certificate	Annual Income

TOTAL:

Bonds: Corporate & Municipal

Face Amount	Company	Purchase Date	Maturity Date	Total Cost	Interest Rate	Current Market Value	Owned by	Location of Book	Annual Income

4. REAL ESTATE (RESIDENCE, RECREATIONAL, INCOME PROPERTY)

Location:	1. 846 Tower Ct.	2.	3.
Date Purchased	7/1/73		
Cost	$50,000		
Current Market Value	$120,000		

5. LIFE INSURANCE

	1.	2.	3.	4.
Insured	Marty	Marty	Marty	
Company	May Insurance Co.	XX2 Ins. Co.	ABC Ins. Co.	
Type of Policy	Term	Whole	Term	
Number of Policy	4638160	5396105	1468014	
Face Amount	$50,000	$25,000	$50,000	
Owner	Marty	Marty	Marty	
Beneficiary	Mary	Mary	Mary	
Cash Value		$2,000		
Amount Borrowed Out		$10,000		
Location of Policy	desk file	desk file	desk file	

6. ANNUITIES, PENSIONS, PROFIT SHARING PLANS, INDIVIDUAL RETIREMENT ACCOUNTS

Description	Participant	Company or Institution	Benefits	Present Value
pension plan	Marty	Big-Little Co.	retirement	$107,000

7. BUSINESS INTERESTS

Company Name	Type of Business	Percentage of Ownership	Value of Your Interest

8. CREDIT OBLIGATIONS

Real Estate (Residence, Recreational, Income Property)

	1.	2.	3.
Mortgage Holder	First Bank		
Mortgage Balance	$26,145		
Interest Rate	8%		
Monthly Payment	$270		

Other Debt Obligations (automobile loans, education loans, life insurance loans, home improvement loans, etc.)

Lender	Type of Loan	Interest Rate	Balance Due	Monthly Payment	Co-signer
State Bank	Auto	12.5%	$5,500	$155	
First Bank	home improvement	8%	$4,560	$95	

Credit Cards:

Name of Card	Number of card	Balance Due
Master Card	838457	$75
Visa	596922	$75
American Express	7704210	$50

Worksheet V: Example
Mr. & Mrs. Mid
LOCATION OF OTHER IMPORTANT PAPERS

Homeowner's Insurance _in desk file_

Name of Company _World Insurance_ Policy Number _O 989-02-82_

Automobile Insurance _in desk file_

Name of Company _World Insurance_ Policy Number _7450-20-221879_

Medical Insurance _at work_

Name of Company _The Blue_ Policy Number _000B63 8919_

Type of Policy _Major Medical_

Location of card _wallet_ Group Number _45106_

Disability Insurance _at work_

Name of Company _American_ Policy Number _369847_

Last Will _at lawyer's_

Codicils _____

Birth Certificates _safe deposit box_

Mortgage Papers or Lease _safe deposit box_

Deeds to Real Estate _safe deposit box_

Titles to Automobiles _safe deposit box_

Military Discharge Papers _safe deposit box_

Citizenship Papers _____

Divorce Decree _____

Social Security Cards _wallet_

Income Tax Returns _desk file_

Worksheet II: Yours
RECORD-KEEPING
Personal Information

Yourself:

1. Name_____ Address_____

    City/State_____ Telephone Number_____

    Place of Birth_____ Date of Birth_____

    Social Security #_____ Marital Status_____

2. Spouse's Name_____ Address_____

    City/State_____ Telephone #_____

    Place of Birth_____ Date of Birth_____

    Social Security #_____

3. Children:

Name	1	2	3	4
Address				
City/State				
Telephone				
Place of Birth				
Date of Birth				
Social Security #				
Marital Status				

4. Parents

    Name_____ Address_____

    City/State_____ Telephone #_____

    Place of Birth_____ Date of Birth_____

    Mother's maiden name_____

5. Spouse's Parents

    Names_____ Address_____

    City/State_____ Telephone_____

    Place of Birth_____ Date of Birth_____

    Mother's Maiden Name_____

    Next of Kin:

    Name_____ Relationship_____

    Address_____ Telephone #_____

    Neighbor or Close Friend

    Name_____ Address_____

    City/State_____ Telephone_____

Worksheet III: Yours
Personal Contacts

	NAME	ADDRESS	TELEPHONE NUMBER
Attorney			
Accountant			
Clergyman			
Stockbroker			
Physician			
Trust Officer			
Banker			
Life Insurance Agent			
Other Insurance Agents			
Homeowner			
Automobile			
Medical			
Disability			
Executor of Estate			
Financial Planner			
Others			

Worksheet IV: Yours
RECORD KEEPING

1. CHECKING ACCOUNTS, SAVINGS ACCOUNTS, CREDIT UNION ACCOUNTS, OTHER CASH ACCOUNTS

Name of Institution	Type and # of Account	Interest Rate	Current Balance	Owned By	Location of Checkbook or Passbooks

2. MONEY MARKET FUNDS, CERTIFICATES OF DEPOSIT, TREASURY BILLS AND NOTES

Name of Institution	Type and # of Account	Maturity Date	Amount Invested	Interest Rate	Owned by	Location of Passbooks

TOTAL _____

3. SECURITIES

Stocks & Mutual Funds:

Number of Shares	Company	Date Purchased	Cost	Current Market Value	Owned By	Location of Stock Certificate	Annual Income

Bonds: Corporate & Municipal

Face Amount	Company	Purchase Date	Maturity Date	Total Cost	Interest Rate	Current Market Value	Owned by	Location of Book	Annual Income

TOTAL: _____

4. REAL ESTATE (RESIDENCE, RECREATIONAL, INCOME PROPERTY)

Location: 1. _____   2. _____   3. _____
Date Purchased
Cost
Current Market Value

5. LIFE INSURANCE

	1.	2.	3.	4.
Insured				
Company				
Type of Policy				
Number of Policy				
Face Amount				
Owner				
Beneficiary				
Cash Value				
Amount Borrowed Out				
Location of Policy				

6. ANNUITIES, PENSIONS, PROFIT SHARING PLANS, INDIVIDUAL RETIREMENT ACCOUNTS

Description	Participant	Company or Institution	Benefits	Present Value

7. BUSINESS INTERESTS

Company Name	Type of Business	Percentage of Ownership	Value of Your Interest

8. CREDIT OBLIGATIONS

Real Estate (Residence, Recreational, Income Property)

	1.	2.	3.
Mortgage Holder			
Mortgage Balance			
Interest Rate			
Monthly Payment			

Other Debt Obligations (automobile loans, education loans, life insurance loans, home improvement loans, etc.)

Lender	Type of Loan	Interest Rate	Balance Due	Monthly Payment	Co-signer

Credit Cards:

Name of Card	Number of card	Balance Due

Worksheet V: Yours
LOCATION OF OTHER IMPORTANT PAPERS

Homeowner's Insurance _____

    Name of Company _____ Policy Number _____

Automobile Insurance _____

    Name of Company _____ Policy Number _____

Medical Insurance _____

    Name of Company _____ Policy Number _____

    Type of Policy _____

    Location of card _____ Group Number _____

Disability Insurance _____

    Name of Company _____ Policy Number _____

Last Will _____

Codicils _____

Birth Certificates _____

Mortgage Papers or Lease _____

Deeds to Real Estate _____

Titles to Automobiles _____

Military Discharge Papers _____

Citizenship Papers _____

Divorce Decree _____

Social Security Cards _____

Income Tax Returns _____

THE BAROMETER OF FINANCIAL FITNESS:
YOUR NET WORTH STATEMENT

4

If you will now look at the financial worksheets on pages 29-34, you will find a framework in which to work. It gives you a way of looking realistically at where you are now and a way to plan your Financial Fitness Program for the future.

Here are some tough questions. You can find the answers by filling out the worksheet headed **Net Worth Statement Worksheet** on page 35.

- How much will you have to pass on to your heirs?
- Will it produce enough income for them to survive?
- Are you accumulating enough assets to help support yourself during retirement?
- Should your investments be producing income now or in the future?
- Are you carrying too much debt?
- What about inflation: Are you keeping ahead of it, are you even keeping up with it?

Your Net Worth Statement can tell you where you

stand financially at any given point in time. It's like weighing and measuring yourself before you start a physical fitness program. The definition of net worth? It's the difference between your assets, what you own that has monetary value, and your debts, or what you owe. In short, it's an inventory of everything you own that has any monetary value.

Why go to all this trouble, calculating your net worth? Because it is essential for estate planning, retirement planning, and for any sound investment strategy. Knowing your net worth can give you security both now and in the future. It is also your only way of estimating how much you will have available to pass on to your heirs.

If your Net Worth Statement reveals some negatives—if your net worth is not increasing, if you have taken on more debt than you can handle, if your investments have not kept up with inflation—you can assess what is going on and do something about it. Financial needs do change, remember. Your Net Worth Statement can help you get over the hurdles imposed by change.

How much are things worth?

Now it's time to be objective. As accurately as possible, write down the actual market value of your property, be it your home, your great-aunt's heirloom diamonds, or your automobile. Not what you think your property might be worth, mind, but what it would actually fetch if you were putting it up for sale.

How do you find out what things are worth? Your best bet is to get a dealer or appraiser who knows houses, diamonds, or automobiles—or rare coins, antique dolls, or whatever else you own that is of real value—and have an estimate made.

Talk with a real estate broker about the current market value of your home. And check your local newspaper for advertisements for comparable houses.

It can be tough to get accurate values on personal property. Clothing and furniture and other household furnishings may have depreciated since you purchased them. Silver, gold, stamps, antiques, and coins have probably risen in value since you bought them or inherited them. In some cases, such as coins or antiques, a reputable specialized magazine may include listings you can depend on.

Go back to your record-keeping worksheets for a guide to items to list. The first is cash on hand, in saving or checking accounts. Certificates of deposit due within the coming year, money market funds, stocks, and bonds should all be itemized. A daily newspaper listing will tell you today's market value of stocks, bonds, and mutual funds.

Don't forget the hidden assets:

- Your employee benefits
- Your pension or profit-sharing plan (list present values)
- Life insurance (cash values of whole policies should be listed)
- Your interest in a business partnership or similar venture (list the price you would receive if you sold your share; this is often one's largest asset and the most difficult to appraise).

How much do you owe?

Now for the liabilities. Start with current bills. List everything you have been billed for but have not yet paid, as of today. List any taxes that are unpaid, including all taxes that have not been deducted from your paycheck, federal or state income tax, capital gains tax, real estate taxes, personal property taxes.

Next list the unpaid balance on the mortgage on your home or condominium or vacation house. Itemize installment debts: everything you owe to Mastercard, VISA, American Express, other rotating charge accounts, and your cash reserve account at the bank. Add up unpaid balances on a car loan, home improvement loan, education loan, or life insurance loan.

Got the form filled out? Please check it again. Anything you forgot to list under assets? Any missing liabilities?

Total the assets column, then the liabilities column. Now subtract your liabilities from your assets. The result is your net worth as of right now.

If your liabilities turn out to be greater than your assets, you have a "negative net worth" at the moment. The exercise has been doubly worthwhile for you, for it has drawn your attention to a precarious situation that needs immediate attention.

NET WORTH OF YOUNGS, MIDS, AND ELDERS . . .

When Mr. and Mrs. Young do their Net Worth Statement, it points up the fact that they have not saved anything. Their only investments are their personal possessions. Their incomes are overcommitted to meeting debt obligations.

Their parents, the Mids, have built up their assets by saving. Their home, purchased a number of years ago, has appreciated greatly in value. They have a strong asset in Mr. Mid's pension fund. Compared with many in their situation, they have few large obligations, though they are still paying on their mortgage and have some outstanding credit obligations. The Mids were able to use some of their assets to finance their children's educations.

The Elders have assets in their home, on which mortgage payments have been completed, and in securities. They have almost no liabilities.

Worksheet VI: Example One
Mr. & Mrs. Young
NET WORTH STATEMENT
Date___3 / 1 / 87___

When filling out this form, refer back to Chapter 3, Record-Keeping, Worksheet IV.

ASSETS	Monetary Value	Owner of Asset

Current Assets (see 1. Current Balance, 2, Amount Invested)

Checking Account	$150.	joint
Savings Account	$500.	joint
Credit Union Accounts		
Money Market Funds		
CD's		
Treasury Bills		
Treasury Notes		

Securities (see 3. Current Market Values)

Stocks		
Bonds		
Mutual Funds		

Real Estate (see 4. Current Market Value)

Residence		
Recreational Property		
Income Property		

Long Term (see 5. Cash Value, 6. Present Value, 7. Value of Your Interest)

Insurance		
Annuities		
Pensions		
Profit Sharing Plans		
Individual Retirement Accounts		
Business Interests		

Personal Property	Monetary Value	Owner of Asset
Home Furnishings	$ 5,000	joint
Automobiles	$ 7,000	joint
Clothing & Furs		
Jewelry		
Antiques		
Stamp Collection		
Coins		
Fine Art		
TOTAL ASSETS	$ 12,650	

LIABILITIES OR CREDIT OBLIGATIONS

Current Liabilities:	Amount Due	Obligator
Medical & Dental		
Current Bills	$ 460.	joint
Charge Accounts	$ 400.	joint

Unpaid Taxes

Capital Gain		
Federal		
State		
Local		

Real Estate (see 8.)

Residence		
Recreational		
Income Property		

Other Dept or Installment Debt (see 8.)

Automobile Loans	$ 4,100	joint
Home Improvement Loans		
Education Loans		
Life Insurance Loans		
Margin Accounts		
Bank Loans		
Credit Cards	$ 2,750.	joint

TOTAL ASSETS	$ 12,650.
TOTAL LIABILITIES	$ 7,710.
NET WORTH	$ 4,940.

Worksheet VI: Example Two
Mr. & Mrs. Mid
NET WORTH STATEMENT
Date **3/1/87**

When filling out this form, refer back to Chapter 3, Record-Keeping, Worksheet IV.

ASSETS	Monetary Value	Owner of Asset
Current Assets (see 1. Current Balance, 2, Amount Invested)		
Checking Account	$ 2,000	joint
Savings Account	$ 2,500	joint
Credit Union Accounts		
Money Market Account	$ 20,000	joint
CD's		
Treasury Bills		
Treasury Notes		
Securities (see 3. Current Market Values)		
Stocks		
Bonds		
Mutual Funds		
Real Estate (see 4. Current Market Value)		
Residence	$120,000	joint
Recreational Property		
Income Property		
Long Term (see 5. Cash Value, 6. Present Value, 7. Value of Your Interest)		
Insurance	$ 2,000	husband
Annuities		
Pensions	$ 107,000	husband
Profit Sharing Plans		
Individual Retirement Accounts	$ 4,000	husband
Business Interests		

Personal Property	Monetary Value	Owner of Asset
Home Furnishings	$30,000	joint
Automobiles	$11,000	joint
Clothing & Furs	$5,000	joint
Jewelry	$10,000	wife
Antiques		
Stamp Collection		
Coins		
Fine Art		
Other	boat $5,000	husband
TOTAL ASSETS	$318,050	

LIABILITIES OR CREDIT OBLIGATIONS

Current Liabilities:	Amount Due	Obligator
Medical & Dental	$100	joint
Current Bills	$600	joint
Charge Accounts	$200	joint

Unpaid Taxes

Capital Gains		
Federal		
State		
Local		

Real Estate (see 8.)

Residence	$26,145	joint
Recreational		
Income Property		

Other Dept or Installment Debt (see 8.)

Automobile Loans	$5,500	joint
Home Improvement Loans	$4,560	joint
Education Loans		
Life Insurance Loans		
Margin Accounts		
Bank Loans		
Credit Cards	$850	joint

TOTAL ASSETS	$318,050
TOTAL LIABILITIES	$37,955
NET WORTH	$280,095

Worksheet VI: Example Three
Mr. & Mrs. Elder
NET WORTH STATEMENT
Date___*3/1/87*___

When filling out this form, refer back to Chapter 3, Record-Keeping, Worksheet IV.

ASSETS	Monetary Value	Owner of Asset
Current Assets (see 1. Current Balance, 2, Amount Invested)		
Checking Account	$ 500	joint
Savings Account	$ 5,000	joint
Credit Union Accounts		
Money Market Funds		
CD's		
Treasury Bills		
Treasury Notes		
Securities (see 3. Current Market Values)		
Stocks	$ 21,665	husband
Bonds		
Mutual Funds		
Real Estate (see 4. Current Market Value)		
Residence	$ 28,000	joint
Recreational Property		
Income Property		
Long Term (see 5. Cash Value, 6. Present Value, 7. Value of Your Interest)		
Insurance		
Annuities		
Pensions		
Profit Sharing Plans		
Individual Retirement Accounts		
Business Interests		

Personal Property	Monetary Value	Owner of Asset
Home Furnishings	$10,000	
Automobiles	$2,000	
Clothing & Furs	$10,000	
Jewelry		
Antiques		
Stamp Collection		
Coins		
Fine Art		
TOTAL ASSETS	$77,165	

LIABILITIES OR CREDIT OBLIGATIONS

Current Liabilities:	Amount Due	Obligator
Medical & Dental	$250	
Current Bills	$100	
Charge Accounts	0	

Unpaid Taxes

Capital Gains		
Federal		
State		
Local		

Real Estate (see 8.)

Residence		
Recreational		
Income Property		

Other Dept or Installment Debt (see 8.)

Automobile Loans		
Home Improvement Loans		
Education Loans		
Life Insurance Loans		
Margin Accounts		
Bank Loans		
Credit Cards		

TOTAL ASSETS	$77,165
TOTAL LIABILITIES	$350
NET WORTH	$76,815

Assets and liabilities change continually, of course, almost on a daily basis. You need not redo your Net Worth Statement to reflect weekly or monthly fluctuations. But as your major needs and situations change, the emphasis on assets and liabilities will vary and it will be important to keep an eye on your net worth.

What kinds of major needs and situations are important enough to make you revise your Net Worth Statement? I'd say the following: buying a larger house; inheriting securities; becoming vested in an employee profit-sharing plan; signing for a car or boat or second-home loan; putting savings into an individual retirement account (IRA).

Review your Net Worth Statement at least once a year. It is a barometer of your financial situation. When you are weighing needs, a look at your assets and at your net worth can help you make a sound decision.

Worksheet VI: Yours
NET WORTH STATEMENT
Date_____

When filling out this form, refer back to Chapter 3, Record-Keeping, Worksheet IV.

ASSETS	Monetary Value	Owner of Asset
Current Assets (see 1. Current Balance, 2, Amount Invested)		
Checking Account		
Savings Account		
Credit Union Accounts		
Money Market Funds		
CD's		
Treasury Bills		
Treasury Notes		
Securities (see 3. Current Market Values)		
Stocks		
Bonds		
Mutual Funds		
Real Estate (see 4. Current Market Value)		
Residence		
Recreational Property		
Income Property		
Long Term (see 5. Cash Value, 6. Present Value, 7. Value of Your Interest)		
Insurance		
Annuities		
Pensions		
Profit Sharing Plans		
Individual Retirement Accounts		
Business Interests		

Personal Property	Monetary Value	Owner of Asset
Home Furnishings	_____	_____
Automobiles	_____	_____
Clothing & Furs	_____	_____
Jewelry	_____	_____
Antiques	_____	_____
Stamp Collection	_____	_____
Coins	_____	_____
Fine Art	_____	_____

TOTAL ASSETS _____

LIABILITIES OR CREDIT OBLIGATIONS

Current Liabilities:	Amount Due	Obligator
Medical & Dental	_____	_____
Current Bills	_____	_____
Charge Accounts	_____	_____

Unpaid Taxes

Capital Gains	_____	_____
Federal	_____	_____
State	_____	_____
Local	_____	_____

Real Estate (see 8.)

Residence	_____	_____
Recreational	_____	_____
Income Property	_____	_____

Other Dept or Installment Debt (see 8.)

Automobile Loans	_____	_____
Home Improvement Loans	_____	_____
Education Loans	_____	_____
Life Insurance Loans	_____	_____
Margin Accounts	_____	_____
Bank Loans	_____	_____
Credit Cards	_____	_____

TOTAL ASSETS _____
TOTAL LIABILITIES _____
NET WORTH _____

BUDGET YOUR WAY TO FINANCIAL FITNESS

5

"Budget" is a forbidding word, even frightening to some people. They see it written down or, worse yet, actually say it and their palms begin to sweat.

"Budget." The word does seem to reach down into you, twisting and tightening, just as the word "homework" used to and perhaps "dentist" still does today.

But you can make friends with a budget. It doesn't have to be something you dread. You can draw it to you, make it a part of your life—so much so that the day will come when you will feel lost without it, when you will knock down anyone who tries to take your budget away from you, when it will be as simple and practical and valuable a tool as your checkbook or shopping list.

A budget is a worksheet. A budget is a road map. A budget is a resume. It describes your lifestyle. It tells who you are and where you are and where you want to be.

Today your standard of living is called your lifestyle. But whatever you want to call it, it is simply how you live—the goods and services you spend your money on. Your budget is to Your Financial Fitness Program what your diet is to your physical fitness program.

There are no fixed rules that apply to everyone when it comes to budgeting. One man's hamburger is another man's steak. Variations are endless. Some put their money into cars while their homes fall apart. Some eat well but wear threadbare clothes. Some achieve a nice balance among home, cars, clothing, food, and education for their children. But no one can *tell* anyone else how to spend his or her money. All of us have to decide for ourselves just what our priorities are, for no two individuals, no two families, no two budgets are quite alike. *Your* budget is your own: *your* picture of *your* lifestyle. So you must create it and nurture it.

The budget as a road map

Think of your budget as a road map. Its purpose is

to show you where you are going and how to get there. But like any road map, it can also show you where you can sensibly get off the road, and then get safely back on again without losing direction or missing your destination. That is important. Sometimes you do have to change your route, in order to cope with an emergency or a change in plans that may entail delay in reaching your destination. Nothing wrong with that if you have your map to guide you and remind you of your goal and the route you structured to reach it.

Your budget is the key to knowing how much credit you can safely afford to carry. Often inflation, with its threat of higher prices tomorrow if you don't buy today, has encouraged people not to wait until they can afford to buy. But, for many people, the day of reckoning is at hand. With paychecks stretched to the breaking point, there is no more room for impulsive buying while still paying for yesterday's excesses. And so each of us faces a risk when we want to take on a new credit obligation: Can we really afford the payments? Only a well-tended budget can provide an answer to that question.

THE TIGHT BUDGET OF DOLLY AND JIM YOUNG . . .

The Youngs' average monthly fixed expenses are $943. Of this, 45 percent is in debt reduction. This means they are constantly paying off debt rather than putting some money into an emergency fund.

Their flexible expenses are $1212 per month. Thus, between paying off debt and buying necessities, they are spending almost every dollar that comes into the house.

Taking a good hard look at this situation, they have decided that their first priority must be to pay off current debts without incurring any more. To ease the situation, they will have to cut down on some expenses, making do with the clothes they have now (except for buying clothes for the baby, who is growing by leaps and bounds), and slash entertainment expenses. Jim also will have to cut down his lunch expenses by brown-bagging.

Worksheet VII: Example One
BUDGET

SOURCES OF INCOME
Mr. & Mrs. Young
Yearly

EARNED INCOME	Husband	Wife	Joint	Total	Monthly
Salary & Wages	$27,500	$7,500		$35,000	$2,917
Self-Employment Income					
Bonus					
INVESTMENT INCOME					
Interest on Savings					
Interest from Bonds					
Capital Gains					
Dividends					
Rental Income					
Trust Income					

YOUR PERSONAL FINANCIAL FITNESS PROGRAM

EARNED INCOME	Husband	Wife	Joint	Total	Monthly
PENSIONS & ANNUITIES					
Social Security					
Employer's Pension					
Private Pensions					
Other					
OTHER INCOME					
Family Contributions					
Gifts					
Unemployment, Disability Insurance					
Alimony & Child Support					
Gross Income	$27,500	$7,500		$35,000	$2,917

DEDUCTIONS

EARNED INCOME	Husband	Wife	Joint	Total	Monthly
TAXES					
Federal				$5,200	$433.33
State	1,250	375		1,625	135.41
Local					
SOCIAL SECURITY	1,966	536		2,502	208.50
BENEFITS					
OTHER					
NET INCOME				$25,673	$ 2,139.41

Worksheet VIII: Example One
Mr. & Mrs. Young's FIXED & FLEXIBLE EXPENSES

FIXED EXPENSES	JAN	FEB	MAR	APR	MAY	JUN	JUL	AUG	SEP	OCT	NOV	DEC	TOTAL
1 Rent/Mortgage	385.	385.	385.	385.	385.	385.	385.	385.	385.	385.	385.	385.	$4,620.
2 Fuel													
3 Electricity	25.	30.	30.	29.	25.	34.	50.	64.	58.	25.	20.	25.	415.
4 Telephone	50.	45.	40.	40.	36.	52.	41.	38.	45.	50.	48.	40.	525.
5 Water													
6 Homeowners Insurance				65.						65.			130.
7 Automobile Insurance		110.			110.			110.			110.		440.
8 Disability Insurance													
9 Medical Insurance													
10 Life Insurance													
11 Life Insurance													
12 Life Insurance													
13 Personal Property Tax													
14 Real Estate Taxes													
15 Income Tax													
16 Automobile Loan	282.	282.	282.	282.	282.	282.	282.	282.	282.	282.	282.	282.	3,384.
17 Loan Repayment Furniture	75.	75.	75.	75.	75.	75.	75.	75.	75.	75.	75.	75.	900.
18 Loan Repayment MasterCard	35.	35.	35.	35.	35.	35.	35.	35.	35.	35.	35.	35.	420.
19 Other Debt Visa	40.	40.	40.	46.	46.	40.	40.	40.	40.	40.	40.	40.	480.
20 Emergency Fund													
21 Other													
22													
23 TOTAL FIXED EXPENSES	892.	1002.	887.	951.	988.	903.	908.	1089.	920.	957.	995.	882.	11,314.
24 Monthly Average	943.	943.	943.	943.	943.	943.	943.	943.	943.	943.	943.	943.	
25 Difference (Amount to be set aside for	51.		56.			40.	35.					61.	
26 fixed expense account)													
27													
28													
29													
30													
31													

FLEXIBLE EXPENSES	JAN	FEB	MAR	APR	MAY	JUN	JUL	AUG	SEP	OCT	NOV	DEC	TOTAL
1 Food/Beverage	325.	325.	325.	325.	325.	325.	325.	325.	325.	325.	325.	325.	$3,900.
2 Clothing	175.	200.		60.	55.	250.	150.	15.	250.	75.	120.	120.	1,470.
3 Laundry/Cleaning	8.	10.	4.		55.		6.	5.				8.	96.
4 Home/Office Supplies *Stamps*		5.	9.				15.		18.			25.	72.
5 Animals													
6 Personal Care Toiletries		25.		20.		50.		20.		25.	15.	40.	195.
7 Periodicals *books*	13.	28.	19.	30.	13.	13.	36.	13.	13.	22.	28.	25.	253.
8 Recreation													
9 Entertainment *lunches-meals out*	200.	200.	200.	200.	200.	200.	200.	200.	200.	200.	200.	200.	2,400.
10 Travel/Vacations							600.						600.
11 Gifts		25.		35.		75.						150.	285.
12													
13 **Household Maintenance**													
14 Lawn & Snow Removal													
15 Maid													
16 Garbage													
17 Repairs													
18 Home Furnishings	250.				85.			175.			300.	450.	1,260.
19 Major Appliance Purchases		400.											400.
20													
21 **Transportation**													
22 Gas/Oil	83.	120.	95.	75.	95.	110.	145.	175.	135.	115.	104.	96.	1,348.
23 Repairs		55.		65.		30.			150.				300.
24 Licenses & Registration													
25 Commutation, Parking													
26													
27 **Children's Expenses**													
28 Allowances													
29 Lessons *Babysitting*	25.	40.	35.	40.	30.	35.	30.	45.	40.	45.	35.	50.	450.
30 Camp													
31 Recreation/Sports													

BUDGET YOUR WAY TO FINANCIAL FITNESS

Mr. & Mrs. Young's FIXED & FLEXIBLE EXPENSES

		JAN	FEB	MAR	APR	MAY	JUN	JUL	AUG	SEP	OCT	NOV	DEC	TOTAL
1	Education													
2	Tuition													
3	Room/Board													
4	Books & Supplies													
5	Travel													
6														
7	Medical Expenses													
8	Doctor			150.						200.		75.		425.
9	Dentist	85.						75.						160.
10	Drug				25.			40.			20.		10.	95.
11														
12	Contributions													
13	Church/Synagogue													
14	Other Charity													
15	Savings													
16	TOTAL FLEXIBLE EXPENSES	1,164.	1,433.	837.	875.	858.	1,088.	1,622.	973.	1,331.	827.	1,202.	1,499.	14,546.
17	TOTAL FIXED EXPENSES	860.	970.	855.	919.	956.	871.	876.	997.	888.	925.	963.	850.	11,314.
18	TOTAL EXPENSES	1,974.	2,003.	1,692.	1,794.	1,729.	1,709.	2,478.	1,795.	2,219.	1,752.	1,745.	1,899.	25,860.
19	NET INCOME	1,813.	1,813.	1,813.	1,813.	1,813.	1,813.	1,813.	1,813.	1,813.	1,813.	1,813.	1,813.	25,673.
20	PROFIT (LOSS)													(187)
21														
22														
23														
24														
25														
26														
27														
28														
29														
30														
31														

YOUR PERSONAL FINANCIAL FITNESS PROGRAM

The Gemini budget: getting and spending

All budgets have two sides. One covers revenue, or what comes in. The other covers expenses, or what goes out. These two sides, income and outgo, are basic to every budget ever created, whether it is that of a single person or a giant corporation with worldwide production, employees and sales.

Let's start with your revenue budget. See worksheet VII headed **Sources of Income** on page 55. On this sheet, write down *all* your income for yourself and your spouse by category: what you earn as wages or salary; extra money you take in from part-time work, moonlighting, hobbies, or whatever; interest you get from savings accounts; dividends from investments; rent from property you own or from roomers or boarders; gifts and contributions from family members or others; Social Security or other pension payments; payments from disability or unemployment insurance; tax refunds.

Be honest with yourself. Don't count any unhatched chickens. The raise you've been promised is not income until you see it in your paycheck. Your budget is always what is happening right *now*. It is never what might be.

Expenditures are of two kinds: fixed and flexible.

Fixed expenses are those that you cannot escape or change to any great degree: the mortgage or rent payment, for instance. Insurance premiums, taxes, monthly credit obligations, and utilities also come under this heading. (You can, of course, reduce utility bills somewhat by being careful about telephone usage, turning out lights, and lowering the thermostat.)

Handling fixed expenses

Your most important fixed expense is the toughest to make. It is a payment to yourself for an emergency fund. More about that in a moment.

The second most important expense is payment to a "fixed expenses" account. Many people set up a separate checking account for this purpose. To determine how much to put into this account every month, line up all your fixed expenses for the year. Worksheet VIII headed **Fixed and Flexible Expenses** will help you to work out the details outlined here. Note that you have to pay some expenses every month (rent or mortgage, for example); some quarterly (insurance premiums, probably); some semi-annually (real estate taxes); and some annually (motor vehicle licenses, for example).

Total each category and figure out its monthly average. Then total the monthly averages of all the categories to see how much must go into your fixed-expenses account each month. Hard as it will be— *at first*—you must start immediately to put in that amount every month. (If possible, put it in an interest-bearing account.) And you must resist with every fiber in your body the urge to take that fixed-expenses account checkbook to the supermarket or to a sale. Once you have set the habit, though, it will be easy to maintain. And with the account established and functioning well, you will always be able to pay the tax bill or the insurance premium when it comes due.

An emergency fund is not the same as a fixed-expenses account. Your emergency fund should contain the equivalent of from three to six months' net income. If you and your spouse are young and both working, if car and appliances and house are new and not likely to cry for major repairs soon, it is safe to have a minimum of three months' income stashed away. If you are older, have a large family and many obligations, you will feel a lot more comfortable when you maintain a six-month cushion for emergencies.

This cash reserve is intended for emergencies only, such as a major medical expense not covered by insurance, a major auto or household repair, a stretch of unemployment. Such emergencies, without the reserves ready to pay for them, could send you off to sign for a loan. That in turn would add to your fixed obligations each month, giving you more to pay, more to worry about, and less to have for flexible expenses and discretionary spending.

(If your self-discipline is really strong, you can easily keep your emergency fund in your separate fixed-expenses account; even better, however, is to put it into a separate savings account.)

Important: Think about your emergency fund before you think about an investment program. It takes precedence.

Handling flexible expenses

What are flexible expenses? They are payments you make regularly but which vary in amount depending on what you're doing, how you're feeling, what you need. Food is a major item, of course. Other expenses include clothing; medical care; transportation; entertainment and recreation; household maintenance, such as cleaning services, reupholstering, redecorating or recarpeting; laundry and dry-cleaning; and magazine subscriptions. Worksheet VIII will help you to categorize all these items and more.

THE MIDS: BUDGET UNDER CONTROL . . .

MR. AND MRS. MID have a combined *gross income* of $54,550 including both their salaries and interest on savings. But for budget purposes they must look at their *net income*, which is $40,767. Here's how payroll deductions based on their itemized deductions and personal exemptions reduce their income:

$8,100 Federal income taxes (IRS)
$1,893 State income taxes
+ $3790 FICA (Social Security) (7.15% on maximum of $43,800)
_____
$13,783 total deducted from paychecks

$54,550 gross income to Mr. and Mrs. Mid
- 13,783 payroll deductions
_____
$40,767 net income

Some people have more payroll deductions than the Mids, such as contributions to a pension plan, deductions for a payroll savings plan, union dues, premiums for Blue Cross, major medical, life insurance, and so on, depending on the particular situation.

Worksheet VII: Example Two
BUDGET

SOURCES OF INCOME
Mr. & Mrs. Mid's
Yearly

EARNED INCOME	Husband	Wife	Joint	Total	Monthly
Salary & Wages	$44,000	$9,000		$53,000	$4,416.67
Self-Employment Income					
Bonus					
INVESTMENT INCOME					
Interest on Savings			$1,550	$1,550	$129.17
Interest from Bonds					
Capital Gains					
Dividends					
Rental Income					
Trust Income					

EARNED INCOME	Husband	Wife	Joint	Total	Monthly
PENSIONS & ANNUITIES					
Social Security					
Employer's Pension					
Private Pensions					
Other					
OTHER INCOME					
Family Contributions					
Gifts					
Unemployment, Disability Insurance					
Alimony & Child Support					
Gross Income	$44,000	$9,000	$1,550	$54,550	$4,545.83

DEDUCTIONS

EARNED INCOME	Husband	Wife	Joint	Total	Monthly
TAXES					
Federal				$8,100	$675
State				$1,893	$157.75
Local					
SOCIAL SECURITY	$3,146	$644		$3,790	$315.83
BENEFITS					
OTHER					
NET INCOME				$40,767	$3,397.25

Worksheet VIII: Example Two
Mr. & Mrs. Mid's FIXED & FLEXIBLE EXPENSES

	FIXED EXPENSES	JAN	FEB	MAR	APR	MAY	JUN	JUL	AUG	SEP	OCT	NOV	DEC	TOTAL
1	Rent/Mortgage	270	270	270	270	270	270	270	270	270	270	270	270	3,240
2	Fuel	241	182		278					75			222	998
3	Electricity	80	45	50	60	50	40	75	110	125	75	50	50	810
4	Telephone	53	30	32	26	43	50	41	33	34	50	38	46	475
5	Water	45						20						65
6	Homeowners Insurance	220												220
7	Automobile Insurance	324						324						648
8	Disability Insurance													
9	Medical Insurance													
10	Life Insurance													
11	Life Insurance	150						150						300
12	Life Insurance			125						125				250
13	Personal Property Tax													
14	Real Estate Taxes			600						600				1,200
15	Income Tax													
16	Automobile Loan	155	155	155	155	155	155	155	155	155	155	155	155	1,860
17	Loan Repayment	95	95	95	95	95	95	95	95	95	95	95	95	1,140
18	Loan Repayment													
19	Other Debt													
20	Emergency Fund													
21	Other													
22														
23	TOTAL FIXED EXPENSES	1633	777	1327	883	613	610	1130	663	1479	645	608	638	11,206
24	Monthly Average	934	934	934	934	934	934	934	934	934	934	934	934	
25	Difference (Amount to be set aside for		157		51	321	324		271		289	326	96	
26	fixed expense account)													
27														
28														
29														
30														
31														

46

Mr. & Mrs. Mid's FIXED & FLEXIBLE EXPENSES

	FLEXIBLE EXPENSES	JAN	FEB	MAR	APR	MAY	JUN	JUL	AUG	SEP	OCT	NOV	DEC	TOTAL
1	Food/Beverage	300	300	300	300	300	300	300	300	300	300	300	300	3,600
2	Clothing	85	175	40	300	80	40	190		200		40	150	1,000
3	Laundry/Cleaning	75	30	25	40	20	95	15		25	20		15	360
4	Home/Office Supplies			15		10		25					75	125
5	Animals			50			165			35		50		300
6	Personal Care Toiletries		30	25	60		15		15	40	35	75	50	345
7	Periodicals	12	25	35	40	50	45	35	40	35	40	25	12	394
8	Recreation			100		400								500
9	Entertainment	60	150	125	60	80	100	75	65	95	110	125	150	1,200
10	Travel/Vacations			125			850					125		1,100
11	Gifts		200	50		50	100		50		75		1000	1,525
12														
13	**Household Maintenance**													
14	Lawn & Snow Removal	25	25		75		35		50		80			290
15	Maid													
16	Garbage													
17	Repairs AND PAINTING		50			550				75		125		800
18	Home Furnishings													
19	Major Appliance Purchases													
20														
21	**Transportation**													
22	Gas/Oil	175	200	150	120	105	95	150	80	80	90	105	95	1,445
23	Repairs			75		400	200			75		450		1,200
24	Licenses & Registration		20			10			20		10			60
25	Commutation, Parking													
26														
27	**Children's Expenses**													
28	Allowances													
29	Lessons													
30	Camp													
31	Recreation/Sports													

Mr. & Mrs. Mid's FIXED & FLEXIBLE EXPENSES

		JAN	FEB	MAR	APR	MAY	JUN	JUL	AUG	SEP	OCT	NOV	DEC	TOTAL
1	Education													
2	Tuition	4,500							4,500					9,000
3	Room/Board		450	450	450	450			450	450	450	450	450	4,500
4	Books & Supplies	250							250					500
5	Travel					188			188				375	751
6														
7	Medical Expenses													
8	Doctor													
9	Dentist													
10	Drug													
11														
12	Contributions													
13	Church/Synagogue	60	60	60	60	60	60	60	60	60	60	60	60	720
14	Other Charity				50		175			10			50	265
15	Savings-IRA's				4,000									4,000
16	TOTAL FLEXIBLE EXPENSES	5,992	1,715	1,625	5,255	2,753	3,275	850	6,568	1,980	4,270	1,930	2,782	34,495
17	TOTAL FIXED EXPENSES	1,633	777	1,327	863	613	610	1,130	663	1,479	645	608	838	11,206
18	TOTAL EXPENSES	6,655	2,492	2,952	6,138	3,366	2,885	1,980	5,731	2,459	1,915	2,538	3,620	45,701
19	NET INCOME													40,767
20	PROFIT (LOSS)													(4,934)
21														
22														
23														
24														
25														
26														
27														
28														
29														
30														
31														

Mary and Marty Mid's fixed expenses are almost the same as those of their children, the Youngs. The big difference is in their credit obligations—$182 a month less than the Youngs'.

The Mids bought their home in 1973 for $50,000, paying $15,000 down. Their 25-year mortgage on the $35,000 balance demands a monthly payment of $270 for principal and interest. In addition, they pay $1,200 in real estate taxes each year. When Marty reaches retirement age at 65, the house will be free and clear.

The Mids' largest expense right now is for the education of their youngest child. Mary's salary, combined with savings, has made up the difference between their take-home pay and their expenses. Once they have finished with education expenses, they plan to begin an active investment plan for their long-delayed vacation tour and for their retirement.

THE STRAINED BUDGET OF THE ELDERS

Things have not gone as expected for the Elders. They had thought that their retirement income from social security, interest and dividends would stretch further in the sunny southwest. However, expenses have soared since they made the move.

Their fixed expenses seem low compared to the Youngs and the Mids. Yet, over half of these expenses go to pay ever increasing utility bills. Food, transportation and unreimbursed medical expenses cut into over half of their flexible expenses. Little is left for vacations, dining out and a little fun. They are going to have to take a look at their assets to see if they can make ends meet.

Worksheet VII: Example Three
BUDGET

SOURCES OF INCOME
Mr. & Mrs. Elder's
Yearly

EARNED INCOME	Husband	Wife	Joint	Total	Monthly
Salary & Wages					
Self-Employment Income					
Bonus					
INVESTMENT INCOME					
Interest on Savings			$425	$425	$35.41
Interest from Bonds					
Capital Gains					
Dividends	$928			$928	$77.33
Rental Income					
Trust Income					

EARNED INCOME	Husband	Wife	Joint	Total	Monthly
PENSIONS & ANNUITIES					
Social Security	$8,568	$3,216		$11,784	$982.00
Employer's Pension					
Private Pensions					
Other					
OTHER INCOME					
Family Contributions					
Gifts					
Unemployment, Disability Insurance					
Alimony & Child Support					
Gross Income	$9,496	$3,216	$425	$13,137	$1,094.75

DEDUCTIONS

EARNED INCOME	Husband	Wife	Joint	Total	Monthly
TAXES					
Federal					
State					
Local					
SOCIAL SECURITY					
BENEFITS					
OTHER					
NET INCOME	$9,496	$3,216	$425	$13,137	$1,094.75

Worksheet VIII: Example Three
Mr. & Mrs. Elder's FIXED & FLEXIBLE EXPENSES

	FIXED EXPENSES	JAN	FEB	MAR	APR	MAY	JUN	JUL	AUG	SEP	OCT	NOV	DEC	TOTAL
1	Rent/Mortgage													600
2	Fuel	65	75	40	30	40	45	55	35	40	40	60	75	600
3	Electricity	50	40	45	40	55	80	90	95	85	50	40	50	720
4	Telephone	75	65	30	40	45	55	40	55	40	35	60	60	600
5	Water	70			65			75			90			300
6	Homeowners Insurance							240						240
7	Automobile Insurance		96			96			96			96		384
8	Disability Insurance													
9	Medical Insurance		125			125			125			125		500
10	Life Insurance													
11	Life Insurance													
12	Life Insurance													
13	Personal Property Tax													
14	Real Estate Taxes	90			90			90			90			360
15	Income Tax													
16	Automobile Loan													
17	Loan Repayment													
18	Loan Repayment													
19	Other Debt													
20	Emergency Fund													
21	Other													
22														
23	TOTAL FIXED EXPENSES	350	401	115	265	361	180	590	406	165	305	381	165	3704
24	Monthly Average	309	309	309	309	309	309	309	309	309	309	309	309	
25	Difference (Amount to be set aside for			194	44		129			144	304		124	
26	fixed expense account)													
27														
28														
29														
30														
31														

BUDGET YOUR WAY TO FINANCIAL FITNESS

	FLEXIBLE EXPENSES	JAN	FEB	MAR	APR	MAY	JUN	JUL	AUG	SEP	OCT	NOV	DEC	TOTAL
1	Food/Beverage	250	250	250	250	250	250	250	250	250	250	250	250	3000
2	Clothing	110		20		20		50			75		25	300
3	Laundry/Cleaning													
4	Home/Office Supplies													
5	Animals		40				100			25	75			240
6	Personal Care Toiletries	20	20	40		15	50	35	40	10		10		240
7	Periodicals	15	15	35	10	12	20	30	15	18			10	180
8	Recreation													
9	Entertainment Meals - Movies	20	35	35	65	45	25	55	20	45	40	65	75	520
10	Travel/Vacations											200		200
11	Gifts	15		50			55		30		15		295	455
12														
13	**Household Maintenance**													
14	Lawn & Snow Removal													
15	Maid													
16	Garbage													
17	Repairs		25		50	30		110		15		40		230
18	Home Furnishings					30			50					80
19	Major Appliance Purchases													
20														
21	**Transportation**													
22	Gas/Oil	85	100	90	120	65	110	70	65	100	130	125	120	1200
23	Repairs			250				145	85	65		120		600
24	Licenses & Registration													
25	Commutation, Parking													
26														
27	**Children's Expenses**													
28	Allowances													
29	Lessons													
30	Camp													
31	Recreation/Sports													

		JAN	FEB	MAR	APR	MAY	JUN	JUL	AUG	SEP	OCT	NOV	DEC	TOTAL
1	**Education**													
2	Tuition													
3	Room/Board													
4	Books & Supplies													
5	Travel													
6														
7	**Medical Expenses**													
8	Doctor	300		250	50		50	150	125	25		40		990
9	Dentist		25		150	50			180			75		480
10	Drug			50					45			25		120
11														
12	**Contributions**													
13	Church/Synagogue													
14	Other Charity													
15	Savings													
16	**TOTAL FLEXIBLE EXPENSES**	815	510	1076	695	487	660	925	840	583	635	855	775	8,850
17	**TOTAL FIXED EXPENSES**	350	401	115	265	361	180	590	406	165	305	381	185	3,704
18	**TOTAL EXPENSES**	1,165	911	1,185	960	848	840	1,515	1,246	748	940	1,236	960	12,554
19	**NET INCOME**													13,137
20	**PROFIT (LOSS)**													583
21														
22														
23														
24														
25														
26														
27														
28														
29														
30														
31														

Your best guide to how much money you will need each month to meet these flexible expenses is last year's spending record. If you have no records for last year, start *today* to keep records for the future.

You pay for each expense in one of three ways: with cash, by check at the time of purchase, or by charge account paid later. Always get a receipt, whether you are paying by cash, check or charge. If you cannot get a receipt—not even a cash register tape—make your own note of date, item, and amount. Note the sales tax, too; it's handy for computing sales tax totals when you do your income tax return.

Put all your receipts on a spindle at home, or in large envelopes, filed chronologically. Keep charge receipts on the spindle or in the envelopes, too. When you pay by check, be sure your checkbook stub notes what the purchase was and for whom it was made. Each month, categorize on your charge accounts what is actually charged, not what you are paying on your charge bill as you may be paying it off in installments.

Now add up all the columns. Are your total expenditures higher than your income? Don't be discouraged if they are. Overspending prods you into making a cash flow analysis—the way being overweight forces you to diet. Here are some questions to ask yourself.

- Do we need all these magazines we subscribe to? Are we reading them all?
- Should we eat out as often as we do?
- Does the dog (or the cat, or the bird) really need gourmet food?
- Can we buy in larger quantities, storing extra supplies of non-perishables that we can buy on sale or at a discount, and thus reduce unit costs?
- How much can we save if we cut back on recreation and entertainment?

A close look at cash flow and overspending can change your lifestyle. So can the births of children or their reaching school age or going off to college. If both husband and wife work after a child arrives, the budget must include child care. If private schooling is preferred, the budget must be adapted. New interests—travel, hobbies, golf or tennis or swim clubs—can change the budget, too. So never think of your budget, or your lifestyle, as set in concrete.

One of the biggest budgetary traumas is suffered by the recently married couple, living to the hilt on two incomes, who suddenly realize that a family will put a severe strain on their spending habits.

Do you really need it?

When you want to buy something, ask yourself the question: "Do I really need this?" What the experts call "purchase analysis," the question tends to put the clamp on impulse buying, for, having taken a good hard look at your priorities as you analyze your cash flow, you find yourself distinguishing between buying for pleasure and buying for need. Unless you make this distinction every time you make a significant expenditure—and only you know what's significant for you—you are *not* financially fit.

There's a good way to test whether you really need to buy something. Instead of buying it, first write out a check to yourself for its purchase price. Look at the check. Do you need that amount in order to buy groceries or pay a department store bill? If you do, you don't need that item now. Can you make up the amount by skipping several trips to the movies, by putting off buying that special book, by postponing a holiday trip? Better to do so than to find that you cannot pay for basic flexible expenses, or that you are dipping into money you need for fixed expenses (not so likely to happen if you have set up a fixed-expenses account and are leaving *that* checkbook in the desk when you go shopping).

What about cost effectiveness?

Another good habit of the financially fit: Figure out the cost effectiveness of the goods or services you are buying. These days there is no need to purchase items that you use only rarely, for you can rent almost anything—cars, appliances, furniture, special clothing, camping gear, ski equipment, party dishes and tableware.

Smart grandparents whose grandchildren live too far away to visit more often than a few times a year are better off renting a crib or high chair when they are needed. Smart couples now think twice about owning two cars. With today's gasoline, insurance and maintenance costs, alternatives such as car pooling, riding public transportation, or renting a

YOUR PERSONAL FINANCIAL FITNESS PROGRAM

second car only when necessary can make excellent sense.

By carefully controlling your expenditures, you can actually increase the amount of money you have available to invest for intermediate and long-range objectives. Think of this as profit—the difference between income and the cost of doing business.

To summarize: "Budget" will not be a dreaded word if you let yourself think positively and practically about your lifestyle—what you want to be and how you want to live—and how much money you have available to provide that style. Recognize that Financial Fitness can only be achieved by tracking your spending habits and knowing where the money goes. Formulate judgments about what is important and how you may want to shift your priorities. Create your own road map that shows how you are going to reach your destination. Stick to it unless there is good reason to detour.

There will come times when you must detour in order to pick up assistance, when you must ask for credit. "Credit" is a pleasant, friendly word. One of its synonyms, though, is "debt": a dreaded word. The next chapter will tell you about debt—how to get into it and how to get out again safely and successfully.

IMPORTANT BUDGETING DON'TS

- Don't be dictatorial. Work out the budget by agreement with other family members.

- Don't be in a hurry. You can't do it in an hour or a single sitting. It takes time.

- Don't go by what others spend (that is, don't keep up with the Joneses).

- Don't expect miracles. A budget is a tool to help you manage more effectively. By itself, it will not give you more money or cut your spending.

- Don't nickel and dime it. Round figures up or down to the nearest dollar, and big figures to the nearest ten dollars.

- Don't overdo the paper work. Report the essentials, that's all.

- Don't be inflexible. Remember that a budget must have room for give and take: Circumstances change. The kids will grow, demands will shift, income as well as outgo will change. Be ready to review, evaluate, revise and adjust as your lifestyle changes.

Worksheet VII: Yours
SOURCES OF INCOME

EARNED INCOME	Husband	Wife	Joint	Total	Monthly
Salary & Wages					
Self-Employment Income					
Bonus					
INVESTMENT INCOME					
Interest on Savings					
Interest from Bonds					
Capital Gains					
Dividends					
Rental Income					
Trust Income					

EARNED INCOME	Husband	Wife	Joint	Total	Monthly
PENSIONS & ANNUITIES					
Social Security					
Employer's Pension					
Private Pensions					
Other					
OTHER INCOME					
Family Contributions					
Gifts					
Unemployment, Disability Insurance					
Alimony & Child Support					
Gross Income					

DEDUCTIONS

EARNED INCOME	Husband	Wife	Joint	Total	Monthly
TAXES					
Federal					
State					
Local					
SOCIAL SECURITY					
BENEFITS					
OTHER					
NET INCOME					

Worksheet VIII: Yours
FIXED & FLEXIBLE EXPENSES

	FIXED EXPENSES	JAN	FEB	MAR	APR	MAY	JUN	JUL	AUG	SEP	OCT	NOV	DEC	TOTAL
1	Rent/Mortgage													
2	Fuel													
3	Electricity													
4	Telephone													
5	Water													
6	Homeowners Insurance													
7	Automobile Insurance													
8	Disability Insurance													
9	Medical Insurance													
10	Life Insurance													
11	Life Insurance													
12	Life Insurance													
13	Personal Property Taxes													
14	Real Estate Taxes													
15	Income Taxes													
16	Automobile Loan													
17	Loan Repayment													
18	Loan Repayment													
19	Other Debt													
20	Emergency Fund													
21	Other													
22														
23	**TOTAL FIXED EXPENSES**													
24	Monthly Average													
25	Difference (Amount to be left in													
26	fixed expense account)													
27														
28														
29														
30														
31														

	FLEXIBLE EXPENSES	JAN	FEB	MAR	APR	MAY	JUN	JUL	AUG	SEP	OCT	NOV	DEC	TOTAL
1	Food/Beverage													
2	Clothing													
3	Laundry/Cleaning													
4	Home/Office Supplies													
5	Animals													
6	Personal Care Toiletries													
7	Periodicals													
8	Recreation													
9	Entertainment													
10	Travel/Vacations													
11	Gifts													
12														
13	**Household Maintenance**													
14	Lawn & Snow Removal													
15	Maid													
16	Garbage													
17	Repairs													
18	Home Furnishings													
19	Major Appliance Purchases													
20														
21	**Transportation**													
22	Gas/Oil													
23	Repairs													
24	Licenses & Registration													
25	Commutation, Parking													
26														
27	**Children's Expenses**													
28	Allowances													
29	Lessons													
30	Camp													
31	Recreation/Sports													

		JAN	FEB	MAR	APR	MAY	JUN	JUL	AUG	SEP	OCT	NOV	DEC	TOTAL
1	**Education**													
2	Tuition													
3	Room/Board													
4	Books & Supplies													
5	Travel													
6														
7	**Medical Expenses**													
8	Doctor													
9	Dentist													
10	Drug													
11														
12	**Contributions**													
13	Church/Synagogue													
14	Other Charity													
15	Savings													
16	**TOTAL FLEXIBLE EXPENSES**													
17	**TOTAL FIXED EXPENSES**													
18	**TOTAL EXPENSES**													
19	**NET INCOME**													
20	**PROFIT (LOSS)**													
21														
22														
23														
24														
25														
26														
27														
28														
29														
30														
31														

HOW TO GET INTO DEBT (THE RIGHT WAY) AND OUT AGAIN

6

"If I wait until I can afford it, the price will be even higher."

"Fly now. Pay later."

"No money down. No payment for 90 days."

"Dear Mrs. ———: With the convenience of cash reserve banking, you can write a check even when you have no money in your account . . ."

Sound familiar? These phrases are symptomatic of the easy-credit world we have lived in for the past 30 years.

Credit has been so easy, in fact, that its abuse has become a major problem in the last few years and one of the principal reasons why so few of us are financially fit. Buying has become excessive, and impulsive, as Mr. and Mrs. America (not to mention Ms. America) have enjoyed an incredible spending spree.

Paychecks have been stretched—and stretched again—to and beyond the breaking point. Spending habits have been established, reinforced, and expanded until buying has become such second nature that it can scarcely be brought under control.

Credit is nothing new. Shakespeare knew creditors so well he brought Shylock to life for all time. (Debt is older than Dickens, who depicted debtor's prison well over a century ago.) But *consumer credit*, as we know it, did not really come about in this country until 1856, when Isaac Singer hit upon the idea of time payments ($5 down and $5 a month) to sell his $125 sewing machines at a time when the average American's annual income was $525.

Singer's idea generated sales that never could have been achieved if people had been forced to pay cash. It took a few generations for the idea to become commonplace, but eventually buying big-ticket items "on time" and paying for them while you used them became an American standard. (It also created an industry—bank loan departments, credit unions, General Motors Acceptance Corporation, loan sharks, and myriad others—with millions of employees.)

By the way, credit, as discussed in this chapter, means credit as handled by the kinds of organizations mentioned above. Mortgages are not involved.

Then came the all-purpose credit cards. Diner's Club was the first. When it started in 1950 the total outstanding debt of the American consumer stood at $21.5 billion. Thirty years later—with American Express, VISA, Mastercard, and many others vying with Diner's Club—the figure had reached over $300 billion.

Renting money

What is credit? It is a means of renting money when you need it, and for as long as you need it. It is just as practical as renting a trailer or a floor sander or extra tables and chairs for a party. Rental firms charge you a rental fee. Credit institutions charge you interest. When interest rates rise, you pay the lender more for the money you borrow—just as you would pay more for the trailer or sander if the rental company raised its rates.

IN OVER THEIR HEADS . . .

Dolly and Jim Young have the same problem many others have: They have piled up too much debt. Paying off $432 a month means that they use 20 percent of their net income for debt reduction—too high a ratio for them, especially when they are trying to save to buy a house. (See Worksheet X on page 71) They must work to keep the debt level no higher than 15 percent, or about $297 per month.

The Youngs will have the furniture store paid off in ten months. It would then be easy for them to take the $75 they now pay for furniture and use it for ordinary living expenses. However, if they keep their debt reduction level at $432 a month for 16 months, they will have all debt paid off—and can start a solid saving plan.

Therefore, the best thing for them to do, when the $75 is no longer needed to pay the furniture store, is to apply it to reducing their VISA and Mastercard accounts.

Getting credit—and using it

If you have never borrowed money or bought anything on credit, how do you get credit in the first place?

It's a "Catch 22" situation. You can't get credit until you prove you can be depended on to pay your debts, and you can't prove you can pay your debts

until someone takes the risk of extending credit to you.

If your are a young couple applying for your first credit card, or a woman who has always relied on her husband's credit, you may have a tough time at first. A lender will probably ask you to fill out an application form (see exhibit 2) that is very much like the **Net Worth Statement** (Worksheet VI) and **Sources of Income Statement** (Worksheet VII) in this book. The creditor is looking for three things:

1. Do you have the ability to repay? What is your present total income, including such sources as alimony, child support payments, investments, and part-time employment?
2. What are your assets? Again, your Net Worth Statement lists them and their value.
3. Do you have the willingness to pay? If you have no previous history of repayments, this is the "Catch 22."

If you have no credit history, the lender may insist on a co-signer. Recently I requested a credit card for my daughter, in her own name. She does not yet have enough income to qualify for the card, so I was asked to be a co-signer for her. My income and credit history were used, in effect, to enable her to qualify. This means that I am as liable for payments on her account as she is, but the card is in her name and will be reported as such. Thus she will begin to establish a credit identity of her own.

If you are refused credit on your own the first time you apply, and cannot find a co-signer, what can you do? Try these suggestions:

- Open a checking account at a local bank in your own name. Be sure not to get overdrawn. Get to know your banker. Let him or her get to know you.
- Apply for a charge account at a local store. Pay it promptly.
- Apply for a small bank loan, even if you don't need it. Put the money in a savings account. Withdraw enough each month to make the payments on the loan.
- Establish an installment loan at a local store, purchasing something on time (as distinguished from simply charging).
- Try obtaining a credit card (Mastercard or VISA) through the bank where you have established your checking account and where the banker now knows you and knows you are trustworthy.

Exhibit 2 page 1

CREDIT APPLICATION   **INDIVIDUAL**

Financial Statement Of ___4/1/87___
                              Date

Name: ___Dolly & James Young___   Home Phone No.: ___(303) 623-3671___

Home Address: ___1480 North St.   Denver, Colorado 20068___

Social Security No.: ___044-56-0334___ Age: ___26___ Number of Dependents: _____1_____

Occupation: ___Salesman___   Business Address: ___Rocky Mountain Rd.___

To: State Bank, Denver, Colorado

For the purpose of procuring credit and/or any other accommodations or benefits which may be requested, direct or otherwise, from you from time to time, the undersigned hereby furnishes you with the following as being a true and correct statement of the financial condition of the undersigned and of all facts herein set forth, and for such purpose agrees that you may at any time assume that the condition and affairs of the undersigned have continued and are substantially as good as herein set forth and that there has been no change materially reducing the ability of the undersigned to pay all claims and demands against the undersigned, unless you are notified in writing to the contrary by the undersigned, and for such purpose the undersigned further agrees immediately to notify you in writing of any substantial change in the condition or affairs of the undersigned.

In consideration of the granting of such credit, the undersigned agrees that if the undersigned at any time stops payment, makes a bill of sale, a mortgage, assigns any accounts or transfers of a considerable portion of the undersigned's property without due notice to you, or should the undersigned's stock be attached, or should the undersigned make an assignment for the benefit of creditors, or should a petition in bankruptcy be filed by or against the undersigned or if any of the representations made below prove to be untrue, or if the undersigned fails to notify you of any material change as before agreed; then in any of such cases all of the undersigned's obligations held by you shall immediately become due and payable without demand or notice, and the same may be charged against the balance of any deposit account kept by the undersigned with you, the undersigned hereby giving a continuing lien upon such balance of deposit account from time to time existing to secure all obligations of the undersigned held by you.

It is further agreed that the exercise of or omission to exercise such option in any instance shall not waive or affect any other or subsequent right to exercise the same.

ASSETS		LIABILITIES AND NET WORTH	
Cash on hand and in banks (A)	$ 650.	Notes due Bank (A)	$
Marketable Securities (B)		Notes due Relatives & Friends (G)	
Other Securities (C)		Notes due Others (G)	
Accounts & Notes Receivable		Accounts or Bills Due (G)	7,360.
Relatives & Friends			
Others (D)		Income Taxes Due	
		Other Taxes Due	
Real Estate (E)			
Automobiles	7,000.	Real Estate Mortgages Payable (E)	
Cash Value—Life Ins. (F)		Brokers Margin Accounts	
Other Assets (Describe)		Other Debts (Itemize)	
home furnishings	5,000.	Total Liabilities	$ 7,360.
		Net Worth	$ 5,260.
Total Assets	$ 12,650.		

CONTINGENT LIABILITIES		ANNUAL INCOME	
Endorser, Co-maker, Guarantor	$	Salary	$ 35,000.
Surety		Commissions & Bonuses	
On Contractual Obligations		Dividends & Interest	
Legal Claims		Rent (Net of Expense)	
Other—List		Other Income:	

Other Income:
YOU ARE NOT REQUIRED TO DISCLOSE INCOME FROM ALIMONY, CHILD SUPPORT, OR MAINTENANCE PAYMENTS. HOWEVER, IF YOU ARE RELYING ON INCOME FROM ALIMONY, CHILD SUPPORT OR MAINTENANCE PAYMENTS AS BASIS FOR REPAYMENT OF THIS OBLIGATION, PLEASE COMPLETE THIS SECTION.

(A) Cash in Banks and Notes Due to Banks (Specify If Joint)

Name of Bank	On Deposit	Due Banks	Maturity	Collateral (if any)
State bank	$ 150.	$		
State Bank	500.			

Form MS-1056 Rev 9/78 BB

Exhibit 2 page 2

(B) Marketable Securities

No. of Shares or Face Value (Bonds)	Description	Registered Owner	Cost	Market Value
			$	$

(C) Other Securities

No. of Shares or Face Value (Bonds)	Description	Registered Owner	Cost	Market Value
			$	$

(D) Accounts and Notes Receivable

Borrower and Address	When Due	Balance Due	Original Amount	Collateral (if any)
		$	$	

(E) Real Estate

Description	Date Acquired	Cost	Title in Whose Name	Present Value	Mortgage Amount	Monthly Payment	Mortgage Holder
		$		$	$	$	

(F) Life Insurance

Face Value	Insuror & Address	Owner	Beneficiary	Cash Surrender Value	Loans
$			$	$	

(G) Notes and Accounts Due

Owed to & Address	Balance Due	Payment Terms	Collateral
State Bank	$ 1620.		
Mid Town Bank	2160.		
Main St. Furniture Store	750.		
Visa	1000.		
Master Card	1000.		
Bills	860.		

The undersigned further represents that there are no encumbrances against any of the foregoing property except those specifically disclosed above.

James Young
_____
Signature

Dolly Young
_____
Signature

_____
Date

YOUR PERSONAL FINANCIAL FITNESS PROGRAM

Look at the situation from the point of view of the lending institution—the bank, store, American Express, Diner's Club, whatever. It is concerned with its own risk. It is taking a chance on you, based on your current income and circumstances. (By the way, your loan application should not show income that is based on overtime pay or moonlighting. What if that income ceased? Also, do you have enough emergency funds to carry you and pay your debts if you are laid off? What about a contingency for a large medical expense? All these are factors you should be thinking about when you apply for credit.)

Once you have acquired credit, remember that it is an obligation. You have agreed to pay back the money, and credit must not be abused. Your monthly obligation to repay the debt should be listed as a fixed expense on your budget sheet. Repay it just as you pay your rent or your utilities.

You are now building up a credit record. Next time you seek credit, the lender may obtain a "credit report" on you from a credit bureau. (See Exhibit 3) The report lists all your accounts, noting whether payments have been made on time and are current. It may also include civil suits, judgments against you that were awarded to creditors, and other information that might affect the lender's opinion of you as a credit risk. Note that credit bureaus do not make judgments. They do not rate any consumer's credit history or ability to repay. They only provide information that banks, department stores, gasoline companies, and other companies use to help determine whether the applicant is worthy of credit.

The credit report also shows whether there is a billing problem—from the seller's point of view. For example, if you are disputing a charge by a store and have refused to pay until the matter is settled, or if a former spouse fails to pay his or her own debts, the credit report may show such items as unpaid debts. You are permitted to add up to 150 words to the report to tell your side of the story. This becomes part of your permanent credit record. (Your record is maintained as "permanent" for seven years; bankruptcies, however, are kept on the record for ten years.)

Under the law, you are entitled to see any credit report on you that has been prepared by a credit bureau and to challenge any items in the report that seem incorrect. The credit bureau is obligated to make an investigation and correct any errors. This is especially important if the information or evidence is misleading.

Any time you are denied credit by any organization to which you have applied, you are entitled to receive a copy of your credit history free of charge. If you simply want to check into what a local credit bureau has on you in its files, the bureau may insist on a fee for issuing a copy of your report. Usually the fee is less than $10.

THE MIDS—AND CREDIT . . .

Mary and Marty Mid never got into the "buy now, pay later" syndrome. Both were raised with conservative ideas about money. Over the years, they have borrowed only to buy automobiles and to build the addition to their home, so they are carrying less than 10 percent of take-home pay in credit obligations. The result is that they have no monthly juggling act to see who gets paid next, they do not have to debate whether they can afford to go out to dinner or a movie, and finding education funds for their children has never produced headaches.

Budget: key to credit

To use credit without setting up a working budget is foolhardy. Your budget tells you how much credit you can safely afford. People get into trouble when they don't check to see how much they can carry each month in credit repayments. They get overextended. Then when they run out of money they use credit cards or charge accounts to continue buying items that should be included in regular living expenses.

The scenario goes like this. Checking account balance—zero. Cash in wallets and purses—zero. Need to buy something—use credit. Balance in charge account and on credit cards—rising monthly. Payment each month—a minimum part of the total bill. Balance reaches approved limit—apply for additional credit (in the case of charge cards) or go to other stores and open new accounts.

Eventually the minimum payments plus the finance charges on a number of accounts get to be a major expense, cutting even further into each

Exhibit 3 page 1

TRW CREDIT DATA   UPDATED CREDIT PROFILE   CONFIDENTIAL

INQUIRY INFORMATION

TCR2

DFD2 9999999ABC YOUNG JAMES ., 1825 H 90027, P-2234 W 92667,
S-548926847, M-1825 1842 NORTH DENVER, CO 20018

PAGE 1	DATE 9-11-86	TIME 15:19:14	PORT AL11	H V A14	CONSUMER		02-999999/99

JAMES YOUNG 1842 NORTH DENVER, CO 20018	2-80 A & B SALES 1350 4TH STREET DENVER, CO 3388338	SS# 044-56-0334 YOB-1960

ACCOUNT PROFILE			SUBSCRIBER NAME/COURT NAME			SUBSCRIBER #/COURT CODE	ASSN CODE			ACCOUNT NUMBER/DOCKET		PAYMENT PROFILE NUMBER OF MONTHS PRIOR TO BALANCE DATE
POS	NON	NEG	STATUS COMMENT	DATE REPORTED INQUIRY	DATE OPENED	TYPE	TERMS	AMOUNT	BALANCE	BALANCE DATE	AMOUNT PAST DUE	1 2 3 4 5 6 7 8 9 10 11 12
		A	ABC BANK CURR WAS 30	12/14/86	12/2/84	AUT	2 36	$4,860	$1,944	402245 1/1/87	$162	C1CCCCCCCC11
		A	XYZ BANK CURR WAS 30-3	12/14/86	1/1/84	AUT	2 36	$4,320	$2,160	892939 1/15/87	$120	C1CC1CCC1CCC
	M		FURNITURE STORE CURR ACCT	12/14/86	7/82	CHG	2 REV	$3,000	$750	83844 1/22/87		
A			MASTER CURR ACCT		6/83	CHG	2 REV	$1,500	$1,000	77004 1/25/87		CCCCCCCCCCCC
A			VISA CURR ACCT		6/83	CHG	2 REV	$1,500	$1,000	32214 1/25/87		CCCCCCCCCCCC

© TRW INC. 1971, 1978

Exhibit 3 page 2

NAME OF CREDIT GRANTOR ____________________ TO THE ATTENTION OF ____________________

SIGNATURE: ____________________ DATE: ____________________

EXPLANATION OF INFORMATION ON FORM

TRW *CREDIT DATA* ***UPDATED CREDIT PROFILE*** ***CONFIDENTIAL***

Z				INQUIRY INFORMATION
PAGE	DATE	TIME	PORT	H V
&				

4

ACCOUNT PROFILE 1			SUBSCRIBER NAME COURT NAME 2			SUBSCRIBER # COURT CODE 3	ASSN CODE	AMOUNT	14	ACCOUNT DOCKET NUMBER 5		PAYMENT PROFILE MONTHS PRIOR TO BALANCE DATE 17											
POS	NON	NEG	STATUS COMMENTS 6	DATE REPORTED 7	DATE OPENED 8	TYPE 11	12 TERMS	13	BALANCE	BALANCE DATE 15	AMOUNT PAST DUE 16	1	2	3	4	5	6	7	8	9	10	11	12

1. Information used to obtain this Credit Profile abbreviated in computer language.
2. Your name and most recent address and reporting subscriber number, your employment on the date shown, and year of birth or age, if on file.
3. These columns provide an abbreviated description of the status of the items in your profile. POS(Positive) Generally viewed as favorable by credit grantors. NEG(Negative) Generally viewed as unfavorable by credit grantors. NON(Nonevaluated) May be viewed positively, negatively or indifferently depending on each credit grantor's policy and experience. A and M indicate the method by which the credit grantor reports information to TRW. (M) Manual; Manually prepared form. (A) Automated: Automated tapes prepared from the credit grantor's computer.
4. Name of credit grantor, lienholder or court name.
5. A TRW assigned identification number.
6. An association code describes your legal relationship with an account. (See below)
7. The number assigned to your account by the credit grantor or court docket number.
8. Abbreviated description of the account status. (See Explanation of Status Comments to the right.)
9. The status comment shown in 6 is as of this date.
10. Month account opened or month credit transaction took place. 5-Y or 10-Y indicates open prior to 5 years or 10 years respectively.
11. Credit grantor's abbreviated description of the nature of the credit extended. (See chart below)
12. Terms are the periods within which extensions of credit are to be repaid. Charge accounts are stated as REV meaning revolving. Terms for account types R/E, R/F, R/V and R/C (See #11) are stated in years and for all other account types the terms are stated in months.
13. This amount will be either the amount of the original (or revised) credit established, or the highest amount owed.
14. Balance owning on date stated under balance date (#15) or the name of judgement creditor.
15. Date of the balance (#14).
16. Dollar amount past due on balance date (#15), if any.
17. This information is read from left to right. This column reflects the status of the account for each of the 12 months preceding the balance date (#15). A blank space indicates we do not maintain a payment history of this account. A symbol appearing under one of the numbers (1 through 12) means that the account had such a status (as defined below) in that month under which the symbol appears. The following symbols are used in this column:

C = current
1 = 30 days past due
2 = 60 days past due
3 = 90 days past due
4 = 120 days past due
5 = 150 days past due
6 = 180 days past due
- = no history has been reported for that particular month
Blank = no history maintained, see status comment.

TYPE OF ACCOUNT

ABBREV	EXPLANATION
AUT	Auto
UNS	Unsecured
SEC	Secured
P S	Partially Secured
H I	Home Improvement
FHA	FHA Home Improvement
ISC	Installment Sales Contract
CHG	Charge Account
R E	Real Estate Specific Type Unknown-term in years
SCO	Secured by Co-Signer
BUS	Business
REC	Recreational Merchandise
EDU	Educational
LEA	Lease
COM	Co-Maker (not borrower)
C C	Check Credit or Line of Credit
F C	FHA Co-Maker (not borrower)
M H	Mobile Home
CRC	Credit Card
R F	FHA Real Estate Mortgage-terms are in years
NTE	Note Loan
NCM	Note Loan with Co-Maker
HHG	Secured By Household Goods
H + C	Secured By Household Goods & Other Collateral
ASL	Auto
R V	VA Real Estate Mortgage-terms are in years
R C	Conventional Real Estate Mortgage-terms are in years
R O	Real Estate Mortgage-with or without other collateral Usually a second mortgage-terms are in months Amount shown in $100.00 increments
SLC	Co-Maker (not borrower)
REN	Rental Agreement
SUM	Summary of Accounts with same-status
UNK	Unknown
DCS	Debt Counseling Service
CCP	Combined Credit Plan
QST	Account review by credit grantor
A M	Account monitor by credit grantor
RVW	Account review by credit grantor
EMP	Employment
PSC	Solicitation

ASSOCIATION CODES WITH DEFINITIONS

ASSOCIATION WITH ACCOUNT CURRENTLY ACTIVE . . . . ASSOCIATION TERMINATED AS OF DATE REPORTED

0 . . . . UNDESIGNATED . . . . A
Reported by TRW Credit Data only.

1 . . . . INDIVIDUAL . . . .
This individual is the only person associated with this account.

2 . . . . . JOINT ACCOUNT-CONTRACTUAL RESPONSIBILITY . . . . . B
This individual is expressly obligated to repay all debts arising on this account by reason of having signed an agreement to that effect. There are others associated with this account who may or may not have contractual responsibility.

3 . . . . AUTHORIZED USER-JOINT ACCOUNT C
This individual has use of this joint account for which another individual has contractual responsibility.

4 . . . . JOINT ACCOUNT . . . . D
This individual participates in this account. The association cannot be distinguished between Joint Account-Contractual Responsibility or Authorized User.

5 . . . . CO-MAKER . . . . E
This individual has guaranteed this account and assumes responsibility should maker default. This code only to be used in conjunction with Code 7-Maker.

6 . . . . ON BEHALF OF . . . . F
This individual has signed an application for the purpose of securing credit for another individual, other than spouse.

7 . . . . MAKER . . . . G
This individual is responsible for this account, which is guaranteed by a co-maker. To be used in lieu of Code 2 and 3 when there is a Code 5-Co-Maker.

EXPLANATION OF STATUS COMMENTS

BK ADJ PLN	Debt included in or completed through Bankruptcy Chapter 13.
BK LIQ REO	Debt included in or discharged through
CHARGE OFF	Unpaid balance reported as a loss by credit grantor
CLOS INAC	Closed inactive account
CLOS NP AA	Credit line closed not paying as agreed
COLL ACCT	Account seriously past due account assigned to attorney, collection agency or credit grantor's internal collection department
CO NOW PAY	Now paying, was a charge-off
CR CD LOST	Credit card lost or stolen
CR LN CLOS	Credit line closed reason unknown or by consumer request there may be a balance due
CR LN RNST	Account now available for use and is in good standing. Was a closed account
CURR ACCT	This is either an open or closed account in good standing. If the account is a credit card or charge account, it should be available for use and there may be a balance due. If the account is closed, there were no past due amounts reported and it was paid
CUR WASCOL	Current account was a collection account
CUR WAS DL	Current account was past due
CUR WASFOR	Current account. Foreclosure was started
CUR WAS 30	Current account was 30 days past due
CURWAS30-2	Current account was 30 days past due twice
CURWAS30-3	Current account was 30 days past due three times
CURWAS30-4	Current account was 30 days past due four times
CURWAS30-5	Current account was 30 days past due five times
CURWAS30 - 6	Current account was 30 days past due six times or more
CUR WAS 60	Current account was 60 days delinquent
CUR WAS 90	Current account was 90 days delinquent
CUR WAS120	Current account was 120 days delinquent
CUR WAS150	Current account was 150 days delinquent
CUR WAS180	Current account was 180 days or more delinquent
DECEASED	Consumer deceased
DELINQ 60	Account delinquent 60 days
DELINQ 90	Account delinquent 90 days
DELINQ 120	Account delinquent 120 days
DELINQ 150	Account delinquent 150 days
DELINQ 180	Account delinquent 180 days
DEL WAS 90	Account was delinquent 90 days now 30 or 60 days delinquent.
DEL WAS120	Account was delinquent 120 days now 30, 60 or 90 days delinquent
EDU CLAIM	Claim filed with government for insured portion of balance on an educational loan
FORECLOSURE	Credit grantor sold collateral to settle defaulted mortgage
FORE PROC	Foreclosure proceeding started
INQUIRY	A copy of the credit profile has been sent to this credit grantor at their request
INS CLAIM	Claim filed for payment of insured portion of balance
NOT PD AA	Account not being paid as agreed
PAID ACCT	Closed account zero balance not rated by credit grantor
PAID SATIS	Closed account paid satisfactory
PD BY DLER	Credit grantor paid by company who originally sold the merchandise
PD CHG OFF	Paid account was a charge-off
PD COLL AC	Paid account was a collection account, insurance claim or education claim
PD FORECLO	Paid account. A foreclosure was started
PD NOT AA	Paid account. Some payments were made past the agreed due dates
PD REPO	Paid account was a repossession
PD WAS 30	Paid account was past due 30 days
PD WAS30-2	Paid account was past due 30 days 2 or 3 times
PD WAS30-4	Paid account was past due 30 days 4 times
PD WAS30-5	Paid account was past due 30 days 5 times
PD WAS30 - 6	Paid account was past due 30 days 6 times or more
PD WAS 60	Paid account was delinquent 60 days
PD WAS 90	Paid account was delinquent 90 days
PD WAS 120	Paid account was delinquent 120 days
PD WAS 150	Paid account was delinquent 150 days
PD WAS 180	Paid account was delinquent 180 days or more
REDMD REPO	Account was a repossession now redeemed
REFINANCED	Account renewed or refinanced
REPO	Merchandise was taken back by credit grantor; there may be a balance due
SCNL	Credit grantor cannot locate consumer
SCNL NWLOC	Credit grantor could not locate consumer consumer now located
SETTLED	Account legally paid in full for less than the full balance
TRANSFERRED	Account transferred to another office
VOLUN REPO	Voluntary repossession
30 DAY DEL	Account past due 30 days
30 2 TIMES	Account past due 30 days 2 times
30 3 TIMES	Account past due 30 days 3 times
30 4 TIMES	Account past due 30 days 4
30 5 TIMES	Account past due 30 days 5 times
30 6 + TIMES	Account past due 30 days 6 times or more
30 WAS 60	Account was delinquent 60 days now 30 days

ITEMS OF PUBLIC RECORD

CH 7—FILED	Voluntary or Involuntary Petition in Bankruptcy Chapter 7 - (Liquidation) filed
CH 7—DISCH	Voluntary or Involuntary Petition in Bankruptcy Chapter 7 - (Liquidation) discharged
CH 7—DISM	Voluntary or Involuntary Petition in Bankruptcy Chapter 7 - (Liquidation) dismissed
CH 11—FILE	Voluntary or Involuntary Petition in Bankruptcy Chapter 11 - (Reorganization) filed
CH 11—DISC	Voluntary or Involuntary Petition in Bankruptcy Chapter 11 - (Reorganization) discharged
CH 11—DISM	Voluntary or Involuntary Petition in Bankruptcy Chapter 11 - (Reorganization) dismissed
CH 13—FILE	Petition in Bankruptcy Chapt. 13 (Adjustment of Debt) filed
CH 13—DISM	Petition in Bankruptcy Chapt. 13 (Adjustment of Debt) dismissed
CH 13—COMP	Petition in Bankruptcy Chapt. 13 (Adjustment of Debt) completed
CITY TX LN	City Tax Lien
CITY TX REL	City Tax Lien Released
CONSEL SER	Debt Counseling Service
CO TAX LN	County Tax Lien
CO TAX REL	County Tax Lien Released
FED TAX LN	Federal Tax Lien
FED TX REL	Federal Tax Lien Released
JUDGMENT	Judgment
JUDGMT SAT	Judgment Satisfied
JUDG VACAT	Judgment Vacated or Reversed
MECH LIEN	Mechanic's Lien
MECH RELE	Mechanic's Lien Released
MN MTG FIL	Manual Mortgage Report (Developed credit report prepared for this credit grantor, copy attached.)
NT RESPON	Not Responsible Notice, e.g., husband or wife claims not responsible for debts incurred by spouse.
STAT TX LN	State Tax Lien
STAT TX REL	State Tax Lien Released
SUIT	Suit
SUIT DISMD	Suit Dismissed or Discontinued
WAGE ASIGN	Wage Assignment
W A RELEASE	Wage Assignment Released

COURT CODES

CIR	CIRCUIT
CITY	CITY
CVL	CIVIL
CO	COUNTY
CT	COURT
DIS	DISTRICT
IRS	INTERNAL REVENUE SERVICE
JUS	JUSTICE
MUN	MUNICIPAL
REG	REGISTRAR
ST	STATE
SPR	SUPERIOR
SUP	SUPREME

month's available cash. A monthly payment or two is missed. You start paying each account less than the minimum due. Or you start to juggle, paying this account this month and that account next month. Past due notices begin to come in the mail. Finally a collection agency sends a notice or calls. (See Exhibit 4)

This scenario produces knotted tummies, tense nerves, headaches, ulcers—and a bad credit report. Sometimes it produces total indebtedness that is equal to or greater than your annual income.

The problem crosses all economic and social lines. A $14,000-a-year secretary may owe $14,000. A $100,000-a-year executive may have $100,000 in unpaid debts.

Figuring out your debt ratio

Turn to worksheets IX and X, **Your Lists of Debts** and **Personal Debt Ratio**. Fill in all debts that are current. The total amount of indebtedness is on the Net Worth Statement. Monthly obligations are included under credit repayment on the Fixed Expenses Worksheet.

Exhibit 4

COLLECTION AGENCY NOTICE

YOUR ACCOUNT HAS BEEN PLACED WITH US FOR IMMEDIATE
COLLECTION WITH INSTRUCTIONS FROM OUR CLIENT TO COMMENCE
WITH ALL THE COLLECTION MEANS AT OUR DISPOSAL.

WE ARE PREPARED TO SETTLE THIS ACCOUNT WITHOUT
INCONVENIENCE TO YOU, IF AT ALL POSSIBLE. IT IS IN YOUR
OWN INTERESTS, THEREFORE, TO CO-OPERATE. IF THIS MATTER IS
TO BE SETTLED AMICABLY, WE URGE YOU TO REMIT AT ONCE.
>>>>> USE THE ENCLOSED ENVELOPE TO ENSURE PROPER CREDIT
        TO YOUR ACCOUNT.

* *

* *

Worksheet IX: Example
Mr. & Mrs. Young
LISTS OF DEBTS

Date _____

CREDITOR'S NAME	TYPE OF LOAN	DATE OF LAST PAYMENT	MATURITY DATE	MONTHLY PAYMENT From Budget	TOTAL AMOUNT DUE From Net Worth Statement
1. State Bank	Auto	3/1/87	1 year	$ 162.	$ 1,944.
2. Mid-Town Bank	Auto	3/1/87	1½ years	$ 120.	$ 2,160.
3. Main St. Furniture		up-to-date	10 months	$ 75.	$ 750.
4. Mastercard				$ 35.	$ 1,000.
5. Visa				$ 40.	$ 1,000.

TOTAL MONTHLY PAYMENTS $ 432.

TOTAL AMOUNT OWED $ 6,854.

Worksheet IX: Yours
LISTS OF DEBTS

Date _____

CREDITOR'S NAME	TYPE OF LOAN	DATE OF LAST PAYMENT	MATURITY DATE	MONTHLY PAYMENT From Budget	TOTAL AMOUNT DUE From Net Worth Statement

TOTAL MONTHLY PAYMENTS $ _____

TOTAL AMOUNT OWED $ _____

Now use the Debt Ratio sheet to figure out a ratio for yourself, based on your total take-home pay and your installment obligations. Your debt ratio is a percentage of your take-home pay (the net income you figured out on your budget sheet, after all payroll deductions) that is committed to the repayment of debts.

Most people find that they are in danger if more than 15 to 20 percent of net income is committed to repaying debts. If the ratio goes higher, one is usually robbing Peter to pay Paul: borrowing to meet daily expenses, lengthening the time between payments, charging items that will have a life span less than the time it takes to pay for them.

Here's one good standard to apply: Can all your debts be paid off in 18 to 24 months? If not, your debt ratio is too high.

You should know the ratio of all your debts at any one time. It will change, of course, when you pay off a loan. You can then judge whether it is safe to borrow again, and how much it makes sense to borrow.

Caution: It is easy, when you have just paid off a loan with an obligation of $50 a month, say, to take on another loan with a $65 monthly payment. You think, what's another $15 a month? But if your non-credit expenses are rising along with inflation, that added $15 can be disastrous. Repeatedly adding a new debt that is larger than the one just paid off will slowly but surely put you into a higher and more dangerous debt ratio. Keeping debt within your means, on the other hand, will give you more income for your own security and pleasure. When you are not paying out a large amount for interest, you have more spendable dollars.

Kicking the spending habit: The crash fitness program

When your budget, your cash flow analysis, and

**Worksheet X: Example
Mr. & Mrs. Young
YOUR PERSONAL DEBT RATIO**

Your ratio is based on take-home pay. You have figured out the amount of debt that you owe for installment loans. Is this too much for you?

		Monthly	Yearly
1.	Your total take-home pay	$ 2,139	$ 25,673
2.	Use 20% (maximum for most consumers). Divide income by 5. If you feel this is too high, use 15% or divide by 6.7.	$ 428	$ 5,134
3.	Your present installment obligations	$ 432	$ 5,184
4.	Your present safety margin—subtract line 3 from line 2.	$ (4)	$ (48)
5:	Your personal ratio—divide your installments obligation (line 3) by your take home pay (line 1).	20.20%	20.20%

It might be wise to use both the 15% and 20% figures to see the difference in your own situation.

Worksheet X: Yours
PERSONAL DEBT RATIO

Your ratio is based on take-home pay. You have figured out the amount of debt that you owe for installment loans. Is this too much for you?

		Monthly	Yearly
1.	Your total take-home pay	$	$
2.	Use 20% (maximum for most consumers). Divide income by 5. If you feel this is too high, use 15% or divide by 6.7.	$	$
3.	Your present installment obligations	$	$
4.	Your present safety margin—subtract line 3 from line 2.	$	$
5.	Your personal ratio—divide your installments obligation (line 3) by your take home pay (line 1).		

It might be wise to use both the 15% and 20% figures to see the difference in your own situation.

---

your debt ratio all show that it is time to cut back on expenses in order to pay off debts, you may have to spend a year or so repaying current debts and being scrupulously careful not to add any new ones.

A CREDIT CARD FITNESS TIP

If you have more than one multi-purpose card (VISA, Mastercard, American Express, Diner's Club), it is better to put all large items you charge onto one card. Say you know you are going to pay for a stereo, for instance, over a long time. Why put small items like a shirt or cosmetics on the same card and pay a monthly finance charge on these as well as the stereo? Two multi-purpose cards can be helpful: one for large items not to be paid in full and another for small items that you do pay in full each month. But be careful not to charge large items on the one you intend to pay in full regularly. And be sure that you do pay it in full each month. Otherwise—trouble.

Credit offers many benefits. It allows you to do things and purchase products that you might never be able to do or get otherwise, or that would have taken years to save for. Yet it can be a bane as well. To determine the amount of credit you can comfortably afford to carry, budgeting is a valuable tool. It is the only way to control credit abuse and, if abuse occurs, to take charge and get it back under control.

Either you control credit or credit controls you. It's your choice whether you want to be financially fit.

If you really want to kick the spending habit, your best way to do it is cold turkey. It's tough, but you can do it. Sign an agreement with yourself. Then take all your charge cards and put them in a friend's safe deposit box; or cut them in half and return them to the creditors, with a note of explanation. Look steely-eyed at your budget. Cut out every living expense that is not an absolute necessity and stick to it. Open a separate bank account and put in a certain amount every payday. Use the money in this account for debt reduction and debt reduction *only*.

If you put yourself on this strict regimen, you will achieve Personal Financial Fitness by managing on the amount of money you actually *have*.

Here are some good points to remember on *how to stay out of credit trouble*:

1. Bear in mind that paying a loan is a fixed expense; debt must be paid off.
2. Ask yourself: Would I buy this if I were paying cash? Deferred spending often turns into avoided spending.
3. For smaller purchases, if you can't afford to pay cash, the chances are you can't afford to buy it on credit.
4. Before you decide on a loan, shop around.
5. Avoid impulse shopping or buying something to "lift your spirits."
6. Never use credit for everyday expenses.
7. Keep careful track of credit card purchases, lest you be surprised by an unexpected or unnoticed bill. Everyone in the household who uses credit cards should put the slips in one place immediately after each purchase. Nothing is worse than opening a monthly credit card bill to discover that your spouse has added a large purchase (especially if you happen to think it was an unnecessary one) that you had not anticipated.

HOW TO SEE BANKRUPTCY COMING

To check for real trouble signs, ask yourself:

1. Am I lengthening the time between payments?
2. Am I charging more and more instead of paying cash?
3. Are new bills piling up unpaid?
4. Am I robbing Peter to pay Paul?
5. Am I letting certain bills slide?
6. Am I over my safe ratio of 15 to 20 percent of take-home pay?

Some lending institutions offer to help you by consolidating all your debts. They lend you enough to pay everyone you owe. You then pay them back over an extended period of time.

This type of loan may involve a substantial amount of interest. But it does usually give you a lower monthly payment for debt reduction—lower than

the total of paying all those separate accounts. What you have to watch out for is the simple act of starting to use the plastic cards again while you are still paying off that big loan. If you do start charging, you start the cycle all over again. Almost inevitably, within a few months or a year or two, you will be signing another consolidation loan. The pattern will repeat. This is the path to bankruptcy.

Congress passed the Bankruptcy Reform Act of 1978 to ease the burdens of going bankrupt and to facilitate repayment of a substantial portion of one's debt. The law recognizes the fact that people get themselves into economic situations that are often beyond their control, for the ripple effect of our inflationary economy is especially hard on those who are extended beyond any safety margin. The act has resulted in a tremendous increase in the amount of personal bankruptcy. In 1981, American creditors lost $6 billion through some 450,000 personal bankruptcies.

Before you decide to declare personal bankruptcy, talk with a lawyer. Find out about the various "chapters" of the Bankruptcy Act. You'll learn that petitions have to be filled out, that Chapter 7 covers a "straight bankruptcy" in which the court collects, sells and distributes debtor's assets, with certain exemptions, while Chapter 13 encourages debtors to repay their loans. Chapter 13, the so-called "wage earner plan," allows you to consolidate debts and repay a court-approved percentage of them over three years. Creditors must suspend interest and late charges on most debts, and they are barred from continuing any action against the debtors. If you default on Chapter 13 payments, the court will throw you into Chapter 7 proceedings.

Wise ways with credit

Your credit cards can be the closest thing you will ever have to "free" money. If you understand their billing cycles and how their finance charges are calculated, you can take advantage of them.

The best way to use credit cards is to pay the full amount due every month. Usually a credit card allows a grace period of 25 to 30 days from the date you are billed until you are assessed a finance charge. If you make a purchase immediately after your bill date (which is imprinted on your bill), and if you pay in full when you pay, you can gain free credit for almost two months. For example: Suppose your billing date is July 1. If you buy something on July 2, the purchase will not appear on your bill until August, and you will then have until September 1 (or the stated due date) to pay for it. If you pay the full amount of your new balance by September, no interest will be charged and you will gain free use of your July 2 purchase until the first of September.

Translating and interpreting finance charges

Finance charges will be added to a bill if the amount due is not paid in full. Finance charges may be calculated by a number of methods. The most commonly used is the *average daily balance method*

with newly billed purchases included. This method does not allow the grace period for newly purchased items mentioned in the preceding paragraph. Under this method, it is important to note that the finance charge is based on the average amount you have charged during the month. As soon as your latest purchase goes into the computer, your average changes and your finance charge increases. The finance charge then continues to be calculated on your latest average daily balance until it again changes. Therefore, if this method is used by your creditor, it is better to pay as soon as you receive the bill, rather than waiting (as you might have done when paying in full) until the end of the month. In other words, if you decide to leave part of a bill unpaid for just one month, you will be charged interest. (See Exhibit 5)

Exhibit 5
FINANCE CHARGE CALCULATION

FINANCE CHARGES AS CALCULATED USING AVERAGE DAILY BALANCE WITH NEWLY PURCHASED ITEMS INCLUDED. The finance charge *depends on the date the payment is received* as illustrated. In the first example the payment is made on the 15th of June and in the latter on the 24th. Note there is $1.13 difference by paying it 9 days later.

6/1	Previous Balance	$300.00 × 5	1500.00
6/5	Purchase of $10.00	$310.00 × 5	1550.00
6/10	Purchase of $65.00	$375.00 × 5	1875.00
6/15	Payment of $200.00	$175.00 × 6	1050.00
6/21	Purchase of $18.00	$193.00 × 3	579.00
6/24	Purchase of $7.00	$200.00 × 7	1400.00
		31 days	7954.00

7954.00 divided by 31 (number of days in billing cycle) equals 256.58 (average daily balance) times 1½ equals $3.85 (finance charge).

6/1	Previous Balance	$300.00 × 5	1500.00
6/5	Purchase of $10.00	$310.00 × 5	1550.00
6/10	Purchase of $65.00	$375.00 × 5	1875.00
6/15	Purchase of $18.00	$393.00 × 5	1965.00
6/21	Purchase of $7.00	$400.00 × 6	2400.00
6/24	Payment of $200.00	$200.00 × 5	1000.00
		31 days	10,290.00

10,290.00 divided by 31 equals 331.93   331.93 times 1½% equals $4.98 finance charge

---

Trouble and high finance charges rise together when you make only partial payments month after month. Here's why. Whatever amount you pay, the creditor takes his full finance charge out before deducting anything from the balance you owe. This means that if you pay only the minimum due, you reduce the actual amount you owe only by that amount *less* the finance charge.

Let's say you send in a minimum payment of $50, the amount called for on a hypothetical monthly statement. If the finance charge on the *total* balance you owe is $10, the creditor will take $10 to pay that finance charge and deduct only $40 from the total you owe. If the balance you owe is quite large, your required minimum payment may be mostly interest (or finance charge) month after month and the principal amount you owe will be reduced very, very slowly—much too slowly to be called sound money management.

HOW THE GOVERNMENT WILL CONTRIBUTE TO YOUR FINANCIAL FITNESS: SOCIAL SECURITY BENEFITS

7

"How do I know what I'll get from Social Security?"
"My wife hasn't worked in 35 years—will she get Social Security?"
"How can I be sure they've kept accurate records on me?"
"Is it true that Social Security might not be able to pay everybody it is supposed to in the future?"

Before you can plan retirement or life insurance, you should know what benefits you will be entitled to under Social Security. Few people understand what Social Security is and what it will provide when they retire, or if they become disabled, and what—if anything—it will provide for their dependents when they die.

Just what is Social Security?

It is a program run by the U.S. government to provide continuing income to those whose earnings have ceased because of retirement, disability or death. The program is practically universal, reaching nearly every U.S. citizen. It is a form of social insurance and it is contributory; you and your employer both pay for it while you are working.

Early in your working career, you build up protection until you are a fully insured worker entitled to all the benefits that Social Security provides. This is achieved by earning what Social Security calls "quarters of coverage." The number of quarters of coverage you need in order to draw benefits depends on your age, but once you have 40 quarters of coverage you are fully insured from then on. A quarter of coverage is three months, or a quarter of a year, so 40 quarters is ten years.

Ever changing

The important thing to understand about Social Security is that the amount of benefits available is constantly changing. So is legislation involving Social Security. You must, therefore, view the following figures as examples only and not as the final word. I will show you how to obtain the figures that apply to your own case.

What do you get if you are a fully-insured worker?

When anyone who has contributed to Social Security dies or retires or is disabled, he or she or their dependents are entitled to receive:

- Retirement benefits (a monthly check).
- A monthly payment for a surviving spouse, if 62 or older; if 65, a payment of 50 percent of the spouse's amount, even if the surviving spouse was never employed.
- A monthly payment to unmarried children who are under 18. Children receive 75 percent of a deceased worker's benefit and 50 percent of a retired or disabled worker's, subject to a family maximum.
- A monthly payment to a fully-disabled worker, regardless of age.

What do you get if you are not fully insured?

What if you have less than 40 quarters of coverage, and thus are not fully insured? Then you are what Social Security calls "currently insured." This means that if you die your survivors are eligible for benefits if you have had at least six quarters of coverage in the three years before your death. "Survivors" are qualified dependents: husband or wife, children, and other dependents who qualify.

The "currently insured" status is important to young people who sometimes wonder just what they are getting for their payments into the Social Security system.

How can you tell what your benefits will be?

Your benefits are based on your earnings during all the years you have worked. This figure is on file at Social Security headquarters and is regularly updated. It's a good idea to find out, at least every three years, what your records show. The way to find out is to obtain a Statement of Earnings postcard from your nearest Social Security office or by writing to Social Security Administration, P.O. Box 57, Baltimore, Maryland 21230. (See Exhibit 6)

On the card, fill in your name, address, date of birth, and Social Security number. If you are now over 55, you may include on the card a request for an estimate of your anticipated benefits and for an itemization of your earnings since 1937. (Be prepared to wait some time if you are asking for the latter information.)

Social Security will send you a statement of earnings. (See Exhibit 7) Checking your records is important. If an error occurs, and you wait more than three years, three months and 15 days to report it, it may be too late for a correction. All years prior to the last three are lumped together, so if you do not get the statement of earnings every three years mistakes are difficult to locate and correct. (A file of all your past IRS returns can come in handy for checking purposes.)

The estimate of benefits will help you to determine how much you might receive upon retirement, how much you would receive if you were disabled, and how much your survivors would receive if you died. The estimate may be lower than what you will actually receive at 65. All your earnings covered under Social Security, up to the time you apply for benefits, will be considered in figuring the amount of your retirement benefit. If you have additional earnings covered by Social Security between now and the time you retire, your monthly payment probably will be higher than what we have estimated. With such figures at hand, you can then calculate how much income you will want in addition to Social Security in order to have a comfortable retirement, and how much life insurance you need to protect your dependents.

Estimating your own benefits

You can estimate your benefits yourself, using Social Security tables. Here's how:

Begin with the fact that Social Security uses the average earnings of all workers in each year as a base for its tables. (See Exhibit 8) This is called a wage indexing method. Indexing creates an earnings history which more accurately reflects the value of the individual's actual earnings in comparison to the national average wage level at the time of eligibility. The key to the system is that its "indexing year" is always the second year prior to the worker's "eligibility year." (Those retiring in 1987, for example, use 1985 as the indexing year.) The "eligibility year" is the year a worker turns 62. A person retiring in 1987 would therefore use 1982 as the indexing year (two years prior to the eligibility year of 1984). To make it easier, a retiring worker would use the year of his or her 60th birthday as the indexing year. For disability benefits the eligibility year is either the year the disability begins or the year the worker turns 62, whichever comes first. For benefits for survivors the eligibility year is the year of the worker's death.

Exhibit 6

(Please read instructions on reverse before completing)

REQUEST FOR SOCIAL SECURITY
STATEMENT OF EARNINGS

Your social security number

987	65	4320

Date of Birth

Month	Day	Year
Dec	03	1935

Print Name and Address in ink or use typewriter

Please send a statement of my social security earnings to:

Name _____ Martin Mid _____

Number & Street _____ 846 Tower Court _____

City & State _____ Iowa City, Iowa _____ Zip Code __ 52240 __

Sign Your Name Here _____ Martin Mid _____
                                   (Do Not Print)

I am the individual to whom the record pertains. I understand that if I knowingly and willingly request or receive a record about an individual under false pretenses I would be guilty of a Federal crime and could be fined up to $5,000.

If you ever used a name (such as a maiden name) different from the one above, on a social security card, please print name here:

_____

FORM SSA 7004 PC (3-81)
(PRIOR EDITIONS MAY BE USED UNTIL SUPPLY IS EXHAUSTED)

Exhibit 7
Mr. Mid

Social Security
Summary Statement of Earnings

From: Office of Central Records Operations
Baltimore, Maryland 21235

We are glad to send you this statement of the earnings shown on your social security record. Included are wages you have had for covered employment after 1936 and any earnings from covered self-employment after 1950. This statement does NOT show social security contributions paid.

The statement does not include your earnings for this year (to be reported after the end of the year) and may not include some or all of your earnings for last year because of the time needed to process annual earnings reports. Generally, the statement also does not include earnings over the yearly maximum that can be counted for social security purposes and military service pay before 1957.

If some of your earnings are missing or incorrect, contact any social security office promptly. It is important that your record be correct because entitlement to monthly benefits and Medicare will depend on it. If you wait more than 3 years, 3 months, and 15 days after the year an error occurs, correction may not be possible. Most errors can be reported by phone. If you write or visit an office, submit this statement and furnish proof of the earnings in question (such as a form W-2, pay-slips, or Federal income tax return).

Social Security Number   987-65-4320

YEARS	
1931 thru 1950	NONE
1951 thru 1983	317,100
1984	37,500
1985	39,600
1986	42,000

Based on the date of birth you gave us, you need 40 quarters of coverage to be insured for retirement benefits. Our records show that you now have 40.

Department of Health and Human Services
Social Security Administration

Form OAR-7014a (3-80)

Exhibit 8

SOCIAL SECURITY NATIONAL AVERAGE EARNINGS*

Year	Average Earnings Amounts	Year	Average Earnings Amounts	Year	Average Earnings Amounts
1951	$2,800	1962	4,300	1973	7,600
1952	3,000	1963	4,400	1974	8,000
1953	3,100	1964	4,600	1975	8,600
1954	3,200	1965	4,700	1976	9,200
1955	3,300	1966	4,900	1977	9,800
1956	3,500	1967	5,200	1978	10,600
1957	3,600	1968	5,600	1979	11,400
1958	3,700	1969	5,900	1980	12,500
1959	3,900	1970	6,200	1981	13,700
1960	4,000	1971	6,500	1982	14,500
1961	4,100	1972	7,100	1983	15,200
				1984	16,100
				1985	17,000

*Average earnings are rounded to the nearest hundred.

EXAMPLE: Suppose your indexing year is 1977 and your earnings for 1956 (as shown in Col. 2 of Worksheet B) were $3,000:

$$\frac{\$3,000 \text{ (your earnings in 1956)} \times \$9,800 \text{ (average earnings in 1977)}}{\$3,500 \text{ (average earnings in 1956)}} = \$8,400 \text{ (indexed 1958 earnings)}$$

MR. MID'S BENEFITS . . .

Let's work this out using Mr. Mid as an example. For the moment, suppose Mr. Mid, who was born in 1935 died in 1987.

Since he turned 26 after 1955 we will start his computations with the year 1961, i.e. the year he turned 26.

Step 1. Year of death (eligibility year) **1987**

Step 2. Number of years from 1961 (not including 1987) **25**

Step 3. Indexing year **1985**

Step 4. (See sample Social Security Worksheet on page 83)

Note column 4: The number of years from 1961 through 1986 totals 26. 1986 and 1987 are not indexed. Actual earnings are used. Fill in Columns 3 and 4.

Step 5. Total the figures in Column 4. **729,595**

Note that Column 4 contains 30 years. To equal the Figure in step 2, we eliminate the five years with the lowest figures.

Step 6. Divide the figure in Step 5 by the number of years (2) in Step 2. **29,183**

Step 7. Divide the figure in Step 6 by 12; this figure is your AIME (Average Indexed Monthly Earnings). **2,432**

Step 8. Calculate Primary Insurance Amount. Apply a formula to AIME. The sum of these three separate percentages of the AIME:
90 percent of the first $313 **283.50**

32 percent of the AIME in excess of $313 but less than $1888 ($1,888 − $313 = $1575) **504.00**

15 percent over $1,888 ($2,432 − $1888 = $544 **+ 81.60**

Total **869.10**

Mrs. Mid will not receive any benefits until she reaches age 60. She may then decide whether to start benefits at 60 or at any age until she is 65. If she elects to start receiving benefits at 60, she will get about $622 a month. If she holds off until 65, her monthly payments will be $868.60.

Suppose Mr. Mid did not die in 1987 but was disabled. His monthly check will be $869. Then his wife will receive $323 a month starting when she is 62. However, if she decides to wait until she is 65 to start collecting on his account (and assuming that his account is larger than her own Social Security account) she will receive $434 a month. A woman will not recieve both a wife's benefit and her own old age or disability benefit. If her own benefits are larger than those she would receive as a wife's benefit, she will receive a benefit based on her own record. If her own benefit is less than she would receive as a wife (50 percent of his primary insurance amount at 65) then she will receive the wife's benefit.

There is an advantage for a woman collecting on her own benefit: She will receive it whether her husband is receiving benefits or not. As a wife, however, she can receive only a wife's benefit when her husband starts to collect on his account.

Incidentally, if Mr. Mid wanted to figure out his retirement benefits at this point, on an estimated basis, he could use the figures filled in on the Worksheet XI.

Worksheet XI: Example One
Mr. Mid

Year	1 Social Security maximum earnings base.	2 List earnings in work covered by Social Security (estimates for future years). If earnings are higher than maximum in Col. 1, list the maximum for that year. Insert 0 for no earnings under Social Security.	3 Multiply earnings for each year entered in Col. 2, up to and including your indexing year, by the average earnings for your indexing year (see Table 1) and divide the result by the average earnings for the year being indexed. For years after your indexing year, enter actual earnings you listed in Col. 2, up to the year you plan to apply for benefits.	4 Pick out the highest figures in Col. 3 and enter here. Number of years selected must *equal* number in step 2.	
1953	3,600				
1954	3,600				
1955	4,200				
1956	4,200				
1957	4,200				
1958	4,200	4,200 × 17,000	÷ 3,700	= 19,297	⟩ ELIMINATE
1959	4,800	4,800 × 17,000	÷ 3,900	= 20,923	
1960	4,800	4,800 × 17,000	÷ 4,000	= 20,400	
1961	4,800	4,800 × 17,000	÷ 4,100	= 19,902	
1962	4,800	4,800 × 17,000	÷ 4,300	= 18,976	
1963	4,800	4,800 × 17,000	÷ 4,400	= 18,545	⟩ ELIMINATE
1964	4,800	4,800 × 17,000	÷ 4,600	= 17,739	
1965	4,800	4,800 × 17,000	÷ 4,700	= 17,361	
1966	6,600	6,600 × 17,000	÷ 4,900	= 22,897	
1967	6,600	6,600 × 17,000	÷ 5,200	= 21,577	
1968	7,800	7,800 × 17,000	÷ 5,600	= 23,679	
1969	7,800	7,800 × 17,000	÷ 5,900	= 22,475	
1970	7,800	7,800 × 17,000	÷ 6,200	= 21,387	
1971	7,800	7,800 × 17,000	÷ 6,500	= 20,400	
1972	9,000	9,000 × 17,000	÷ 7,100	= 21,459	
1973	10,800	10,800 × 17,000	÷ 7,600	= 24,158	
1974	13,200	13,200 × 17,000	÷ 8,000	= 28,050	
1975	14,100	14,100 × 17,000	÷ 8,600	= 27,872	
1976	15,300	15,300 × 17,000	÷ 9,200	= 28,272	
1977	16,500	16,500 × 17,000	÷ 9,800	= 28,622	
1978	17,700	17,700 × 17,000	÷ 10,600	= 28,386	
1979	22,900	22,900 × 17,000	÷ 11,400	= 34,149	
1980	25,900	25,900 × 17,000	÷ 12,500	= 35,224	
1981	29,700*	29,700 × 17,000	÷ 13,700	= 36,854	
1982	32,400	32,400 × 17,000	÷ 14,500	= 37,986	
1983	35,700	35,700 × 17,000	÷ 15,200	= 39,927	
1984	37,500	37,500 × 17,000	÷ 16,100	= 39,596	
1985	39,600	39,600 × 17,000	÷ 17,000	= 39,600	
1986	42,000			= 42,000	
1987	43,800			= 43,800	

SOCIAL SECURITY BENEFITS

MR. YOUNG'S BENEFITS . . .

Let's see how the Youngs would make out in the same situations. Suppose Mrs. Young were suddenly widowed and left to raise their one child, or suppose Mr. Young were disabled.

Mr. Young has not yet worked for 40 quarters, so he is not fully insured. He is considered "currently insured" for survivor benefits. At the same time, he is considered fully insured for disability benefits because he has worked in jobs covered by Social Security for half of the quarters since he was 21, and he has not worked less than six quarters since that age.

His figures are:

Step 1. Year of death or disability (eligibility year)   **1987**

Step 2. Years since age 26. (If less than 2, use 2.)   **2**

Step 3. Indexing year.   **1985**

Step 4. (See sample Social Security Worksheet on page 85)

Note that Column 4 contains five years. To equal the figure 2 in Step 2, we must eliminate three years; we cut out the three lowest and use actual earnings for 1981 and 1982, which are the highest. Fill in Columns 3 and 4.

Step 5. Total the figures in Column 4.   **52,500**

Step 6. Divide the figure in Step 5 by the number of years (2) in Step 2.   **26,250**

Step 7. Divide the figure in Step 6 by 12; this figure is your AIME.   **2,188**

Step 8. Calculate Primary Insurance Amount. Apply a formula to AIME. The sum of these three separate percentages of the AIME:

90 percent of the first $313   **281.70**

32 percent of the AIME in excess of $313 but less than $1,888 ($1888 − 313 = $1,575)   **504.00**

15 percent over $1,888 ($2,188 − $1,888 = $300)   + **45.00**

Total   **830.70**

Until the child reaches 16 benefits will total about $1040 per month for both mother and child. Mrs. Young's benefits will then cease, and will not resume until she is either 60 or, if she chooses, 65. If Mr. Young is disabled, the maximum family benefit will be about $1,246.

In the lingo of Social Security, the period when Mrs. Young receives no benefits is called the "blackout period."

Worksheet XI: Example Two
Mr. Young

Year	1 Social Security maximum earnings base.	2 List earnings in work covered by Social Security (estimates for future years). If earnings are higher than maximum in Col. 1, list the maximum for that year. Insert 0 for no earnings under Social Security.	3 Multiply earnings for each year entered in Col. 2, up to and including your indexing year, by the average earnings for your indexing year (see Table 1) and divide the result by the average earnings for the year being indexed. For years after your indexing year, enter actual earnings you listed in Col. 2, up to the year you plan to apply for benefits.	4 Pick out the highest figures in Col. 3 and enter here. Number of years selected must *equal* number in step 2.
1953	3,600			
1954	3,600			
1955	4,200			
1956	4,200			
1957	4,200			
1958	4,200			
1959	4,800			
1960	4,800			
1961	4,800			
1962	4,800			
1963	4,800			
1964	4,800			
1965	4,800			
1966	6,600			
1967	6,600			
1968	7,800			
1969	7,800			
1970	7,800			
1971	7,800			
1972	9,000			
1973	10,800			
1974	13,200			
1975	14,100			
1976	15,300			
1977	16,500			
1978	17,700			
1979	22,900			
1980	25,900			
1981	29,700*			
1982	32,400			
1983	35,700	19,000 × 17,000	÷ 15,200	= 21,250
1984	37,500	21,500 × 17,000	÷ 16,100	= 22,701
1985	39,600	23,000 × 17,000	÷ 17,000	= 23,000
1986	42,000	25,000		25,000
1987	43,800	27,500		27,500

ELIMINATE

Worksheet XI: Yours
AVERAGE INDEXED MONTHLY EARNINGS

Follow these steps to determine your Average Indexed Monthly Earnings (AIME):

Step 1. Enter year you will be 62, or year disability began, or (if survivor is filling this out) year of death. _____

Step 2. Count the years *from* 1955 or the year you were 26, if later, to (but not including) the year in Step 1. _____

Step 3. Determine your indexing year (the year you reach 60, or second year before disability, or second year before death). _____

Step 4. Fill in Social Security Worksheet on page 87. For each year up to and including the indexing year, write down your earnings. (Remember, for this purpose your earnings are only the Social Security maximum for each year, as shown in the worksheet, or less if you earned less; if you made more than $4,200 in 1956, for example, you use $4,200, the maximum for that year.) Follow directions, filling in Columns 3 and 4. _____

Step 5. Total the figures in Column 4. _____

Step 6. Divide the figure entered in Step 5 by the number of years in Step 2. _____

Step 7. Divide the figure in Step 6 by 12; this figure is your AIME. _____

Step 8. Calculate Primary Insurance Amount. Apply a formula to AIME. The formula will depend on your eligibility year. (See below) The sum of these three separate percentages + of the AIME: Total _____

The following are figures for the last four years:

1987 Eligibility Year
  90% of the first $313.00
  32% of any AIME
    above $313.00 to
    $1,888.00
  15% of any AIME over
    $1,888.00

1986 Eligibility Year
  90% of the first $297.00
  32% of any AIME
    above $297.00 to
    $1,790.00
  15% of any AIME over
    $1,790.00

1985 Eligibility Year
  90% of the first $279.00
  32% of any AIME
    above $279.00 to
    $1,680.00
  15% of any AIME over
    $1,680.00

1984 Eligibility Year
  90% of the first $267.00
  32% of any AIME
    above $267.00 to
    $1,612.00)
  15% of any AIME
    above $1,612.00

Worksheet XI: Yours

Year	1 Social Security maximum earnings base.	2 List earnings in work covered by Social Security (estimates for future years). If earnings are higher than maximum in Col. 1, list the maximum for that year. Insert 0 for no earnings under Social Security.	3 Multiply earnings for each year entered in Col. 2, up to and including your indexing year, by the average earnings for your indexing year (see Table 1) and divide the result by the average earnings for the year being indexed. For years after your indexing year, enter actual earnings you listed in Col. 2, up to the year you plan to apply for benefits.	4 Pick out the highest figures in Col. 3 and enter here. Number of years selected must *equal* number in step 2.
1953	3,600			
1954	3,600			
1955	4,200			
1956	4,200			
1957	4,200			
1958	4,200			
1959	4,800			
1960	4,800			
1961	4,800			
1962	4,800			
1963	4,800			
1964	4,800			
1965	4,800			
1966	6,600			
1967	6,600			
1968	7,800			
1969	7,800			
1970	7,800			
1971	7,800			
1972	9,000			
1973	10,800			
1974	13,200			
1975	14,100			
1976	15,300			
1977	16,500			
1978	17,700			
1979	22,900			
1980	25,900			
1981	29,700*			
1982	32,400			
1983	35,700			
1984	37,500			
1985	39,600			
1986	42,000			
1987	43,800			

Exhibit 9
SOCIAL SECURITY BENEFITS AS PERCENTAGE
OF PRIMARY INSURANCE AMOUNT (PIA)

OLD-AGE BENEFIT

Starting age 65 or over .... PIA
Starting age 62-64 .... PIA reduced

DISABILITY BENEFIT .... PIA

WIFE'S BENEFIT (wife of retired or disabled worker)

Caring for child (under 16 or disabled) .... 50% of PIA
Starting age 65 .... 50% of PIA
Starting age 62-64 .... 50% of PIA reduced

HUSBAND'S BENEFIT (husband of retired or disabled
woman worker)

Starting age 65 .... 50% of PIA
Starting age 62-64 .... 50% of PIA reduced

CHILD'S BENEFIT

Child of retired or disabled worker .... 50% of PIA
Child of deceased worker .... 75% of PIA

MOTHER'S OR FATHER'S BENEFIT (widow or widower
caring for child under 16 or disabled) .... 75% of PIA

WIDOW'S BENEFIT (widow not caring for child)

Starting age 65 .... 100% of PIA
Starting age 60-64 .... 100% of PIA reduced

WIDOWER'S BENEFIT

Starting age 65 .... 100% of PIA
Starting age 60-64 .... 100% of PIA reduced

DISABLED WIDOW'S OR WIDOWER'S BENEFIT

Starting age 50-60 .... 50% to 71½% of PIA

PARENT'S BENEFIT (dependent parent of deceased worker)

One dependent parent .... 82½% of PIA
Two dependent parents .... 75% of PIA (each)

Here are some important points to remember about Social Security:

• Until a claim is actually made, the exact amount of benefits can only be estimated. Computations will be reestimated when you file a claim.

• You cannot and will not receive any benefits unless you file for them. Social Security must be notified of your retirement, your disability, or your spouse's death.

• Such notification must be made within six months after the retirement, disability or date of death. The law in almost all cases does not permit any retroactive payment of benefits for a period longer than six months.

• Social Security should be notified at least three months *before* you retire, if you want benefits to start promptly upon your retirement.

• A widow or widower should notify Social Security immediately upon the death of a spouse.

• Survivors of fully-insured and currently-insured workers are entitled to a lump sum benefit of $255; this goes to the wife if she is entitled to benefits or to children if they are the recipients of benefits.

• If you are 65 or over but not yet 70, you may not have earned income totaling more than $8,160 a year or you will lose some of your Social Security benefits. Over 70, there will be no loss of benefits because of employment.

• The amount you are entitled to annually is increased automatically as wage levels rise; it is tied to the Cost of Living Index.

• You should check regularly on what is happening to Social Security rules and regulations and how they affect you.

Once you have established a good estimate of your Social Security benefits, you are ready to talk about life insurance needs and retirement and pension plans.

IS YOUR PENSION PLAN FINANCIALLY FIT?

8

"When can I quality for retirement benefits?"
"When do I have a right to get the money in my pension account?"
"Do I have to pay taxes if I take it all out?"
"Can I move my money to another employer's plan if I change jobs?"

A pension plan is a form of deferred wages. Under some plans, the employer puts in all the money; these are called "non-contributory" plans. In others, the employee puts in some earnings; these are called "contributory" plans.

Of all the workers in the country's private sector (that is, not in government jobs), only slightly more than half are covered by pension plans provided by their employers, whether contributory or non-contributory. There is a bewildering array of basic plans, though, with countless diverse provisions. For our purposes, it is almost impossible to come up with a sample pension plan. So, if your employer offers a pension plan, make a strong effort to become thoroughly familiar with it. Get to know it forwards and backwards, just as you get to know the necessary exercises for your physical fitness program.

There are two basic types of pension plans:

1. *Defined benefit plan.* This type specifies in advance the benefits the retired worker will receive. They may be *either* of the following:

a. *Unit benefit, or percentage rate, plan.* If you have this plan, your benefits are based on your earnings over a specified period of service with the company. The unit may be a specific dollar amount, or it may be a percentage of your earnings. What you get annually is the sum of the benefits credited for each year you were employed. For example, ABC Company pays 1.1 percent of the average *monthly* earnings (counting the highest 60 months out of the last 120) for all years of service for a retiree with average base earnings of $25,000, or $2,083 per month, who has worked for 30 years. The benefit is $687.00 a month.

b. *Flat rate plan.* Here a fixed dollar amount is paid for each year of service. If you receive, for example, $20.25 per month for each year of service, and if you have 30 years of service, you will get $607.50 a month. Often the flat rate plan's rate varies according to job classifications, so those who had better-paying jobs get higher pensions.

2. *Defined contribution plan.* This type is also called an *individual account plan.* The amount of the contributions is fixed. However, the benefits are based on the amount accumulated in an individual's account at the time of retirement. The plan may specify either of the following:

a. *Money purchase plan.* Here, a predetermined formula sets the amount of the contribution. This is a fixed dollar amount each year.

b. *Profit sharing plan.* In this case, the employer's contribution to the plan may vary from year to year as profits of the firm vary.

You should be aware of a number of points when you are contemplating a job and considering the company's pension plan, or when your company offers any change in its existing plans:

• "Vesting" varies. Vesting means that the money credited to your name in the company's pension accounting is legally yours, without question or qualification. Usually you become fully vested only after you have worked a certain number of years or reached a certain age. Three typical vesting situations:

a. No vested right to benefit until five years of employment are completed, at which point you become 100% vested.

b. Partial vesting: under a new seven-year schedule, 20% after completion of the first three years, 20% for each of the next four years until 100% is reached.

HOW MR. MID IS VESTED . . .

Mr. Mid started work at his present company at age 25, under pre-1987 tax law. Consequently, at age 38 he was 50 percent vested, for his age plus seven years

of service equaled 45. At age 43 he was 100 percent vested, having gained another 50 percent at 10 percent a year for the five years from age 38 to 43.

• You are always entitled to all the money you have put in. If your plan is contributory, you may walk away with your share of the contribution before you have any vesting whatever.

• Once you are vested, you may not be forced to forfeit your pension benefits. That money is yours—with very few exceptions. However, many workers do not receive pensions upon retirement because they have not fulfilled the requirements for duration of service. In most firms, the longer you work, the larger your pension. (In our previous example under the flat rate plan, if you have 30 years of service your pension is $607.50 a month; a worker the same age who has been with the company for only 20 years will get $405 per month.)

• Changing jobs can raise problems about vesting. If you move to another job after you are fully vested, the value of your pension will be frozen at the moment when you leave.

You must consider a number of questions:

1. May you take a lump sum distribution and "roll it over" into another form of retirement account?
2. Will you have to pay a tax if you take the lump sum?
3. May you move the money to another employer's pension plan, and will the second employer accept it?
4. May you leave the money with your first employer, and how much will you receive monthly?

Whether you are retiring, or moving to another job and claiming your vested interest in your former company's pension fund, you may have two options in the way your pension is paid to you.

a. *Lump sum distribution.* If you can take the full amount in a lump sum you may "roll it over" into an individual retirement account (IRA) within 60 days after you get it, without having to pay any taxes on it. If you do not roll it over, you will be taxed on the full amount.

The big advantage of lump sum distribution is that you keep control of the money and you decide what type of account you want to put it in. And remember that government securities, savings accounts, money market funds, stocks and bonds, mutual funds, or annuity or endowment contracts are all eligible for IRA roll-over. (See Chapter 11 on Retirement for details on IRA accounts and the various ways assets may be transferred and rolled over.)

b. *Annuity.* A company pension plan must provide an alternative for those who don't want to take lump sum distribution. Most plans call for a joint and survivor annuity to be provided by an insurance company. The annuity automatically pays an employee and his spouse (if they have been married for at least one year) a certain amount. If one dies, the survivor is paid a percentage of the amount that both were getting.

The amount paid each month depends not only on how much the employee or the company, or both, have put into the plan but on the age at which payments are to begin, for it is based on mortality tables. If you start receiving payments at age 65, for instance, they will be smaller amounts than if you wait until age 70 to start. If your spouse is much younger than you, and thus can be expected to live much longer, the monthly payments will be less.

There is another angle that is important to understand: The amount of your monthly check will be higher if you purchase a straight life contract and give up any survivor benefits; this means that if you die, the remaining money that has not been used in payments will revert to the insurance company. You may decide you want a straight annuity paid on your life only. Under some contracts a refund is paid to a beneficiary. If, for instance, an individual dies before receiving total monthly payments that equal or exceed the single premium paid to the insurance company, it will refund the difference to the annuitant's beneficiary.

Under certain conditions it makes good sense to choose a straight annuity paid on your life only. It means that you receive a larger monthly check than if survivor benefits are in the plan. Suppose, for instance, you and your spouse figure out that

with income from Social Security, investments, and proceeds from life insurance policies, she might not need a "survivor" annuity if she were widowed. The income from these other sources would enable her to live quite comfortably. Meantime, while you are alive, you can both profit from the larger pension check. In a word, figure things out. Plan.

What is the advantage of an annuity over a lump sum? You never have to worry about money management, for a start. You are guaranteed a fixed monthly income and you know you will never outlive your capital. Your monthly income will be based upon several things: the amount contributed by your employer and, if the pension plan was contributory, by you; the type of contract, whether single life or joint survivor benefit; and the age at which you begin to receive payments.

But there is a disadvantage to an annuity. Your monthly check remains the same, no matter what inflation does. You have no protection. Inflation can erode the value of your annuity, as many a retired person has learned bitterly in recent years. And there is no changing your mind. Once you have signed the contract and the annuity is paid for, that is it. It has no cash value.

Plan a couple of years ahead

These alternatives, and the seriousness of the consequences of each, make it vitally important that you think your pension plans through with great care well in advance of your retirement. Work on it at least a year ahead. Better yet, two years ahead. Six months before retirement is too late.

As you are working on your plans, many questions will occur to you. Here are the answers to a few of them.

1.   What if you take early retirement? If your pension plan stipulates 65 as retirement age, you are likely to lose one half if you retire at 60 and about two-thirds if you retire at 55.

2.   What if you decide to stay on at work after you reach 65? In calculating pension benefits, most plans do not count the years after 65; that is, most

employers stop contributing after age 65 even if the employee continues to work.

3. What happens to your plan if you take a leave of absence or are laid off temporarily? Check this carefully with your company. For pension purposes, the employer will usually honor all service before and after the break. However, some require a waiting period—usually one year—before you can get back into the plan.

4. Are your pension benefits affected by your Social Security benefits? Do not be surprised if your employer reduces your pension benefit by a percentage of the amount you are getting from Social Security. This can range from 25 percent to as high as 83 percent if you have 30 or 35 years of service. It can be a real shocker.

5. What if you die before you retire? First, your survivors receive a full refund of the money you have contributed to the plan. The law now requires that a pension plan give each participant the option of providing a survivor annuity from the time a married participant becomes eligible for early retirement until he or she retires. In other words, if you die at a time when you are eligible for early retirement, your spouse will receive benefits just as he or she would have if you had already retired and were covered by a joint survivor annuity. The amount of the death benefit may be determined by the amount of pay you were earning at the date of death, or it may be based on the amount of money that has accrued to you in the pension plan.

6. What if you become disabled? Many plans provide for you to become fully vested, regardless of usual vesting rules, if you are permanently disabled. If you are temporarily disabled and unable to work for a while, most plans will hold the benefits that have accrued to you to date. If you have reached early retirement age, you may become entitled to an immediate annuity based on the amount that has accrued in your account up to that date. Some plans provide that a disabled employee may receive early retirement benefits at a younger age, and with fewer years of service, than an able-bodied employee would be entitled to.

7. How do you know the status of your plan?

Legal requirements call for you to be given a summary report on the money in your plan once a year. It is important to be sure that you understand this statement thoroughly. If you have any questions, talk to someone in authority at your place of work who will explain it. Do not just accept the interpretations or guesswork of your fellow workers.

Since it is your retirement, and you want it to be as comfortable as possible, nothing is more important than checking regularly on your pension situation and knowing well in advance just what your benefits will be.

Now that you have looked at Social Security and pension plans, the question is: Will you have enough to live on when you retire? Will you need additional income?

The next step is to look at your assets and see if they can produce more income for you. You may have more alternatives than you think you have.

HOW DOES MARTY MID PREDICT HIS PENSION BENEFITS? . . .

This depends on his years of service with the company. First he works out the average final yearly earnings for his highest-paid 60 months (five years) in the ten consecutive years before he retires. Since he is 13 years away from retirement, the assumption must be made that his income will be at its highest level.

For our purposes, let's take his present salary of $44,000 a year as his average. That means $3,666 a month. When he retires, he will have been with the company for 35 years. The company formula says he is entitled to 1.5 percent of his average monthly earnings, minus 1⅔ percent of his Social Security benefits multiplied by his 35 years of service. So it works out as:

$3,666 × 1.5% × 35 years =	$1,925
less $868 × 1.66% × 3.5 =	-504
	1,421
plus the Social Security	+868
Total income from pension and Social Security	$2,289

If Marty retires earlier, he will lose a certain percentage of his benefits. The company formula gives him 94 percent at age 62, 90 percent at 60, and 75 percent at 55.

We arrived at the $1,421 figure for Marty's pension by assuming he would take his pension in the form of a straight life annuity, which would pay out only as long as he lived.

If he decided to take it as a joint and survivor annuity, things would be different. In this case, the survivor could be either Marty or Mary, and either survivor would continue to receive 50 percent of the payment that came when both were alive. Since the money would now have to stretch further (insurance people, called actuaries, figure all this out from mortality tables), they would get $1,259 while he is alive and the survivor would get $626.

They could also take the annuity as a "ten-year certain." This means that the insurance company guarantees to pay a certain amount for 10 years whether or not Marty lives that long. Thus if he died after only five years, Mary would continue to receive the same amount for another five years. If he lived beyond the ten years, they would also continue to receive the payments. If he dies, however, after the ten-year period ends, Mary would get 50 percent of what he had been getting.

Assuming that Marty and Mary decide they want to take the ten-year certain, his projected retirement income will be:

his Social Security at age 65	$868
her Social Security at age 62	434
the ten-year certain annuity (92.1% of $2,063)	1,308
total income	$2,610

This comes to 71 percent of Marty's present income.

Looking ahead, the Mids have decided that Mary will continue to work as a part-time secretary and they will invest her salary. Since they have more than ten years to go before retirement, and knowing that right now they need little income from investments, they will be careful to make investments that are expected to increase in value and that can be converted into income-producing assets when they retire. All this gives them a hedge against inflation, which they know is likely to cut down on the purchasing power of their projected retirement income.

To accomplish this they will work closely with a professional investment advisor, and they will keep a close watch on their investments. They know the problems the Elders have run into and they intend to avoid the trap of non-involvement.

EVALUATING YOUR ASSETS TO MAKE THEM FIT

9

"How can we get more income from our income-producing assets?"
"Is it costing us too much to maintain our largest non-income-producing asset—our home?"
"Is each of our investments doing the best it can—for us?"
"Those collectibles we have that produce no income: Should we sell some and invest the money?"

These are the kinds of questions that come up when you start evaluating whether your assets meet the Financial Fitness test. Now that you have analyzed your lifestyle and worked out your priorities from your budgeting process, you should begin to consider your assets.

When, or how often, should you evaluate assets? The answer is, every couple of years at least, and more often if you have any major changes in lifestyle, family situation (such as children who have left the nest), or in the assets themselves.

A good reason for not evaluating your assets until now is the fact that assets usually cost you something—unless you inherit them—and it's important to work out your budget first.

Income is the key word when you talk about assets. Some assets produce income. Some do not. Always the hope is that assets that are not producing income right now will keep quietly growing until the day you sell or liquidate them. One hopes they are *appreciating*.

Different needs at various stages of your life dictate what you want assets to do for you. There are times when income from wages or salary is adequate—and times when it is not. When your children are in college or when you are in retirement, income from salary or from a pension may not be enough. Income from assets will then be extremely valuable.

View assets three ways

When you look at assets, you need three viewpoints:

one of your assets, one of your insurance plans, one of your retirement program. If assets are large, insurance plans and retirement programs can be smaller. If assets are small, insurance and retirement programs should be larger. No two cases are alike, so you have to size up all the angles.

If you are like most young couples or young singles, the chances are you have no income-producing assets. The two of you are working, producing two salaries, and spending as much as you can on non-income-producing assets such as furniture, house, or collectibles. So this is the time to buy insurance, while young rates apply, and let cash surrender values start to build up—they will be future assets.

When a young couple makes the commitment to buy their first home, their net worth picture changes dramatically. From this point on, they add to personal possessions with furniture and other household possessions, often without keeping a tight rein on credit. Yet this is the very time when planning should be made for assets that will pay for college expenses in 15 or 20 years. (See Chapter 2 on Goals and Chapter 6 on Credit.)

With income increasing as the family grows in age, size, and number, insurance and its cash values should be looked at every few years. Investments should be watched more closely and bought for growth when the children are young, then realigned to produce more income as the college years approach.

Few people can pay college expenses out of salary. But if you have built up income-producing assets over the years, they can help meet this gigantic expenditure. And, before you start borrowing at high interest rates to pay for college, you may be pleasantly surprised by what you have built up over those 15 or 20 years.

When the kids move out

The empty-nest period brings another change. The years between the end of the children's education and retirement is the time to invest again for growth and appreciation and to make plans for the retirement years. If Mom returns to the work force, two incomes can now help build up the assets, especially with expenses dropping as the children move out on their own. (Surprise! Even the electricity bill drops a little when daughters no longer run hair dryers and stereos are not turned on 24 hours a day). At this point, salaries should once again pay living expenses and leave some extra to build up assets.

The idea now will be to invest for capital appreciation that can be converted into actual income during the retirement years. Credit obligations should be avoided or kept to a minimum.

Now your Net Worth Statement will tell you what your assets are, and your Budget sheets will tell the cost of maintaining them.

There is never any real harm in selling off certain assets. You earned the money to buy them in the first place. You are not stuck with them forever. Must you stay in the same house, for instance, even if it has empty rooms? Now that your children are earning their own way, do you really need the same high insurance coverage you bought when they were in grade school? You have a number of options at this point, many of which we will look at in Chapter 11 on Retirement. For now look at the Elders as an example.

Use the **Asset Evaluation Worksheet** to size up your income-producing and non-income-producing assets.

Income-producing assets

Pick up current assets (checking and savings accounts, securities, and so on) from your Net Worth Statement. (See page 35) Note that except for broker's fees or commissions, these cost you nothing to own or maintain. Fill in annual income from the "sources of income" section of your Budget sheet; yields should come from your Record-keeping sheets.

Non-income-producing assets

Fill in your real estate, personal property, and other long-term assets here. Don't forget such items as fine art and coin and stamp collections. In this area you do have annual costs of ownership: taxes, utilities, and maintenance on the house; premium payments on insurance; insurance premiums on personal property such as a car or boat. The costs of owning these assets come from your fixed expenses budget.

Net sale value is the amount you would get if you sold a particular asset; the market value of your house, for example, minus such costs of selling as real estate commission, legal fees, and so on. There may also be a fee when you sell collectibles.

98

Worksheet XII: Example One
Mr. & Mrs. Elder
ASSETS EVALUATION

INCOME-PRODUCING ASSETS Current Assets	NET SALE VALUE	ANNUAL INCOME (From Budget)	% YIELD (Income ÷ Market Value)	ANNUAL COST OF OWNERSHIP (From Budget)
Checking Accounts	$500	0	0	
Savings Accounts				
Credit Union Accounts				
Money Market Funds	$5,000	$425	8.5%	
Certificates of Deposit				
Treasury Bills				
Treasury Notes				
Securities				
Stocks	$21,665	$928	4.2%	
Bonds				
Mutual Funds				
Total	$27,165	$1,353	4.9%	
NON-INCOME-PRODUCING				
Personal Residence	$28,000			$2,880
Recreational Property				
Cash Value Life Insurance				
Business Interests				
Home Furnishings	$10,000			
Automobiles	$2,000			
Jewelry	$10,000			$1,800
Antiques—Fine Art				
Coin Collection				
Stamp Collection				
Total	$50,000			$4,680

Worksheet XII: Yours
ASSETS EVALUATION

INCOME-PRODUCING ASSETS Current Assets	NET SALE VALUE	ANNUAL INCOME (From Budget)	% YIELD (Income ÷ Market Value)	ANNUAL COST OF OWNERSHIP (From Budget)
Checking Accounts				
Savings Accounts				
Credit Union Accounts				
Money Market Funds				
Certificates of Deposit				
Treasury Bills				
Treasury Notes				
Securities				
Stocks				
Bonds				
Mutual Funds				
Total				
NON-INCOME-PRODUCING				
Personal Residence				
Recreational Property				
Cash Value Life Insurance				
Business Interests				
Home Furnishings				
Automobiles				
Jewelry				
Antiques—Fine Art				
Coin Collection				
Stamp Collection				
Total				

HOW MUCH INSURANCE DO YOU NEED TO BE FINANCIALLY FIT?

10

"How much life insurance coverage do we actually need?"
"The company is buying me Blue Cross—isn't that enough health insurance?"
"Does my homeowner's policy cover my son's stereo equipment at college?"
"How can I cut down on that expensive auto insurance?"

Almost everybody has life insurance of one sort or another, yet few people seem to understand it completely or plan it so they use it to its best advantage. Insurance companies add to the confusion by bombarding us with words and concepts that simply leave us baffled. The "experts" seem to be either super-salesmen who tell us only what they want us to hear, or dodos who have not managed to succeed in other lines of work.

The prime purpose of life insurance is to protect the income part of the budget. It exists to replace the income that stops if the breadwinner dies. But life insurance can also be used for a secondary purpose: to accumulate savings.

The key word in thinking about life insurance is *now*. Now is not ten years ago, and it is not ten years from today. Yet countless people carry life insurance that was right for them ten years ago, or will be right for them ten years from now, but is dead wrong for them now. The fact is that your life insurance needs to be changed as your life changes, and at any given moment you may be overinsured or underinsured. It is important to recognize this and cope with it.

Fortunately, this does not mean that you have to revise your life insurance coverage every year. But if you go more than five years without a thorough review of your needs and coverage, you may be either wasting money on insurance or not buying enough.

The basic types of life insurance

It seems as if each and every insurance company has its own variations on the different types of policies, so it is impossible to describe them all. But here are the basic types:

1. *Term insurance.* This is just what its name implies: You buy life insurance for a specific term, or period of time—usually one to five years. The cost is low; in fact, term is the cheapest form of insurance you can buy. It provides nothing but protection. In other words, it pays off only if you die. It does not build up any savings or other benefits. At the end of the term, you have nothing—but you have had the protection during the term.

If you renew for another term, the cost is higher because you are now older and the likelihood of death is greater as you get older. Usually by the age of 45 or 50, you will find the premium cost for term insurance rising rapidly, much faster than in earlier years. Still, by this age you should either not be buying term or buying less of it.

Term insurance is ideal for a young couple. It provides greater amounts of protection for less money than whole or straight life insurance.

Important: If you are buying term, be sure you get a policy that can be renewed without your having to pass another physical examination. Also be sure it contains a clause that permits you to convert it into a whole policy without a physical exam and at a guaranteed rate. Renewability and convertibility will become important if your health changes. If you become uninsurable or become a high risk, the rate will be prohibitive.

2. *Whole or straight life insurance.* This gives you more than just protection. It includes savings. The amount of the premium is determined by your age and state of health at the time when you buy the policy; it does not increase as long as the policy is in force. Therefore, the younger you are when you buy a whole or straight policy the less it costs you.

During the first few years, the insurance company credits only a small amount to savings. Then, as times goes on, the savings build up. This amount remains yours even if you cancel the policy. Or you can borrow from the insurance company the amount that is in savings, paying interest on it at a rate you will find stated in your policy. If you "borrow against the policy," you continue to pay the premium, thus keeping the policy in force. However, if you die, the insurance company reduces the amount it pays your beneficiary by the amount you borrowed. For exam-

ple, if you have a $25,000 policy but have borrowed $8,000 on it, the company will pay only $17,000.

This "policy loan" provision is a valuable right. It enables you to draw upon the "cash value" that has built up in your policy in order to meet financial needs.

Which to buy—term or whole life?

Many people today question which is better. They wonder if the savings aspect of whole life is worth it. Since it takes a number of years to build up a sizable cash value, the savings are eroded by inflation. So you must ask yourself whether there are other ways to build up savings more quickly and with a greater return, that is, interest or dividends paid on the amount saved.

Ask yourself: How much coverage do I really need now? How much can I afford? Am I being sold on a whole or straight life insurance policy when I need greater protection and could buy it for the same amount of money by taking a term policy? In other words, you must understand what your individual needs are at each point in your life.

THE YOUNGS NEED PROTECTION . . .

Jim and Dolly Young have discussed the fact that protection is their first need now. When they have a second child, they will need more protection, so income would be replaced if Jim died and Dolly would not have to return to work while her children were very young.

THE MIDS HAVE USED CASH VALUES . . .

Having built up savings in insurance while their children were of school age, the Mids were able to borrow substantial amounts to help pay college expenses. Now, with only one child still in college, their financial responsibilities will soon begin to decrease and their need for life insurance will also decrease.

THE ELDERS NEED LITTLE INSURANCE . . .

But it is hard to convince their generation. Many people of this age continue to pay premiums on policies they no longer really need. (See Chapter 11 on Retirement for a discussion of their options.)

How to decide how much you need

The important thing when buying life insurance is to determine how much you need, and buy no more than that. How do you determine the amount? Worksheets are the only way. You must also refer back to the worksheets on Budget, Asset Evaluation, and Social Security and Pension Benefits.

With insurance on your mind, look at your budget sheets. What income will be available for the family if you die?

- Spouse's income, if he or she works or can return to work.
- Social Security payments, if the spouse is eligible for them.
- Income from dividends and interest from investments (see your Asset Evaluation Worksheet).
- Benefits from a pension plan.
- Proceeds from insurance already in force or included in coverage at your place of employment.

Now look at the expense side of your budget. Which expenses will decrease for the rest of the family if you die? Probably food, clothing, transportation, and life insurance premiums. Usually a family needs at least 75 percent of previous take-home pay in order to cover expenses and maintain its lifestyle. Imagine how tough it would be to plan insurance needs accurately if you did not have a good picture of what it costs you to live!

In addition to replacing income, it is a good idea to figure out the cash requirements that insurance should cover in the event of the death of the bread-winner. Some you have already listed in the liabilities column on your Net Worth Statement. Be sure to include:

- Mortgage, installment loans, current bills and other debts.

- Education expenses. If your children are near college age, you will have to calculate more closely than if they are younger. (At current rates, allow $10,000 per year for each child, and multiply by four years.) If the children are younger, it would be hoped that if an insurance policy had to pay off, the amount earmarked for college could be invested at a rate of return that would keep up with the ever-increasing costs of college.

- Final expenses. These include administration of the estate, probate costs, attorney and accountant's fees, appraisal fees, taxes, final unreimbursed medical expenses, and funeral expenses. Rule of thumb: Allow 2 to 5 percent of the total estate, plus up to $5,000 funeral expenses, to cover these.

With so many variables, you can see how the amount of insurance you need can change as life changes. So reevaluate your needs at least every five years to account also for charges in inflation and taxes. And remember: Financial Fitness doesn't mean being overinsured. Careful planning can give you the amount of coverage you need—not the amount an agent wants to sell you. Your Net Worth Statement, Budget, and Asset Evaluation forms have helped you to learn which assets will produce income, which liabilities should be paid off with insurance, and what it will cost you to maintain your lifestyle.

How to handle the proceeds?

When an insured person dies, the insurance company may pay out the policy in any of several ways, known as *settlement options*. The choice may be specified in the insurance policy. However, this is an unfair method because it is impossible to know in advance, when the policy is created, what will best serve the family's needs later on. The intervening years can change too many things. So a decision on the choice of settlement options should not be made when the policy is bought.

By the same token, the decision does not have to be made immediately after the death of the insured person. The insurance company can hold the proceeds of the policy until the beneficiary makes the decision. If you are making that decision, do not be rushed into it. And do not let anyone else make it for you. Here are the options:

1. *Lump sum.* This means you get a check immediately for the full amount of the policy (less any amount that may have been borrowed out). If you have alternate investments, and if you are knowledgeable about investing (or have good advice and are willing to learn), this is a good option. When interest rates are high, the lump sum settlement offers many advantages for you should be able to get a better return on investment than the insurance company provides.

2. *Interest only.* This means the insurance company holds the principal amount but pays you the interest it is earning. This is a good holding position while you decide what to do with the proceeds.

3. *Fixed installments.* At stated intervals, you receive a check for a fixed amount until the money is all used up. The company also pays interest on the remaining balance it is holding.

4. *Fixed period.* The company agrees to pay you the proceeds, plus accrued interest, over a certain period of time. The size of each check depends on the amount of time that the proceeds are spread over.

Important tips:

• If you choose the fixed installment or fixed period option, be sure you have the right to change your mind and withdraw the entire sum at any later date.

• If you choose an annuity, check out what is available from your insurance company versus other annuity contracts. Get the highest monthly income possible for each $1,000 you spend.

• Paying off the mortgage may *not* be the best thing to do, even if you have enough proceeds from the insurance policy to do so. The money you will use to pay it off might be invested at higher rates of interest. If the mortgage has been established for a long time, monthly payments are probably small, with little left to pay, and the rate of interest is probably low. So take a good close look at the mortgage situation and use the money the best way.

What about life insurance for women?

Traditionally, life insurance has been sold to cover the male breadwinner. But with changing roles come changing attitudes. Many women should be covered.

The single woman with no dependents has little need for life insurance. Probably she gets basic coverage as a fringe benefit with her job. This would cover final expenses if she died. More important is disability coverage, to maintain her lifestyle if she cannot work.

The wife and mother who has a job probably needs some life insurance, especially in a family that is dependent on two incomes to maintain its lifestyle. If her children are still young, insurance should be provided to replace her income and cover the added burden of child care. Again, a group policy where she works probably would cover immediate cash requirements, but would not replace income.

The single mother who works and is the sole support of her children must have life insurance. Whether widowed or divorced, if she maintains a career and a household she needs coverage until the children are no longer dependent on her.

Few people ever think of a homemaker providing services to her family that would otherwise cost dollars and cents. Yet that is what she does: cooking, cleaning and child care must all be maintained to keep the family going, and these services will have to be paid for if she is not there. In addition, the expenses of a major illness and of a funeral should be considered—but seldom are.

To anticipate the insurance needed, both immediate and future needs should be considered. Immediate needs include the funeral and settling of the estate. Future needs include housekeeping and child care for a number of years. This will take some calculation. Figure the monthly cost in dollars, multiply by 12 months and then by the number of years before the children will be on their own.

Business partners need insurance

Many a widow finds herself left with a small business. Family and business life may have been intertwined, and probably the business is the largest asset that she and her husband possessed, or that the remaining partner or partners possess.

Life insurance is the key to protecting the business asset, insuring its stability and continuation if a partner or major shareholder dies. It can provide the funds for the surviving members of the business to purchase the share owned by the partner who died, thus saving his widow the possible nightmare of trying to take up where her husband left off, and saving the partners from the possible embarrassment of not having enough money to buy her out.

The amount of insurance coverage should be equal to the partner's or shareholder's interest in the business, and should be formalized in a buy-sell agreement among the partners.

In the case of a business owned by a single individual, life insurance can provide a widow with money to live on while the business is liquidated, again saving her the complications of taking over a business she may not understand, or want to be in, but which provides her livelihood.

KEY POINTS
ABOUT LIFE INSURANCE

In summary, remember these points about life insurance:

1. Buy whole life, or cash value, insurance if you want the premium to stay the same and if you want to build up savings.

2. Buy term insurance if you want maximum protection. Be sure the policy is renewable and convertible.

3. Shop around. Costs and policy terms vary.

4. If possible, take advantage of group insurance. It costs less than an individual policy. Check at your place of work.

5. Remember that your life insurance program is not carved in granite. Review your needs regularly—at least once every five years—recalculating your income and expenses and deciding whether you need more or less coverage. Always match your coverage to your needs.

WHAT IF MARTY MID DIED NOW . . .

How would Mary Mid be left? She would get no monthly Social Security payments yet, for she is not old enough and she has no dependent children still under her care. She would have the income from the savings and money market fund money she and Marty put away.

If Mary took Marty's $125,000 life insurance policy in a lump sum and invested it at an interest rate of 10 percent, she would get $12,500 a year from that.

Under his pension plan, she would get 50 percent of his accrued benefit, since he has been with the company for more than 20 years. (The company plan pays no death benefits to those under 55 who have less than 20 years of service; the widows of those over 55 receive 50 percent of the accrued benefits.)

Here is a formula to work out exactly what share of his pension Mary can expect after Marty's 22 years with the company:

$3,666 (Marty's average monthly earnings × 1.5% [the company formula]) × 22 (Marty's years with the company) = 1,210, 1,210 × 75 percent (the share Marty is entitled to at age 55) = $907.50, $907.50 divided by 2 (Mary is entitled to one-half) = $453.75)

So Mary would get $453.75 monthly from Marty's pension plan if she became a widow now.

Based on these figures, she could work out her needs: If she continues to work part-time and counts her other income from Marty's pension, their savings, and the life insurance, she will have $28,495 of income—or $17,206 short of her needs. To make up this difference would call for $172,060 in investments producing interest at a rate of 10 percent. Looking at the worst side, she might also have more cash requirements for the last year of their youngest child's education, final expenses following Marty's death, and paying off the mortgage and other loans, all of which could mean she needs an additional $219,565 in insurance. (See page 106)

However, looking at the brighter side, the money market fund does contain enough savings for that last year of college, so the education expense can be dropped from the budget. That drastically reduces the need for more insurance. (See page 107)

Worksheet XIII: Example One
Mr. Mid
HOW MUCH LIFE INSURANCE?
(With Education Expense)

A. ANNUAL FAMILY LIVING COSTS (from Budget form) $ 45,701

B. SOURCES OF INCOME AVAILABLE

• Spouse's Income ___ $ 9,000 ___

• Social Security Benefits ___ 0 ___

• Income from Income-Producing
Assets (from Budget form) ___ $ 1,550 ___

• Income from Proceeds of Existing Life Insurance Policies
(use an assumed rate of interest)

6%—multiply amount of insurance by .06
8%—multiply amount of insurance by .08
10%—multiply amount of insurance by .10

___ $125,000 ___ × .10 = $12,500

• Other Sources of Income *(pension)* $ 5,445

TOTAL SOURCES OF INCOME $ 28,495

C. ADDITIONAL INCOME NEEDED (subtract B from A) $ 17,206

D. AMOUNT OF MONEY TO MAKE UP SHORTAGE
(at an assumed rate of interest)

6%—multiply by 6
8%—multiply by 8
10%—multiply by 10

___ $ 17,206 ___ × 10 $ 172,060

E. ADDITIONAL CASH REQUIREMENTS

Final Expenses ___ $ 7,500 ___

Education for Children ___ INCLUDED IN ANNUAL FAMILY COST ___

Liabilities (including Mortgage) ___ $ 37,005 ___ $ 47,505

F. INSURANCE NEEDS (D plus E) $ 219,565

Worksheet XIII: Example Two
Mr. Mid
HOW MUCH LIFE INSURANCE?
(Without Education Expense)

A. ANNUAL FAMILY LIVING COSTS (from Budget form) $ 35,450

B. SOURCES OF INCOME AVAILABLE

- Spouse's Income $ 9,000

- Social Security Benefits 0

- Income from Income-Producing Assets (from Budget form) $ 1,550

- Income from Proceeds of Existing Life Insurance Policies (use an assumed rate of interest)

  6%—multiply amount of insurance by .06
  8%—multiply amount of insurance by .08
  10%—multiply amount of insurance by .10

  $ 125,000 × .10 = $ 12,500

- Other Sources of Income $ 5,445

  TOTAL SOURCES OF INCOME $ 28,495

C. ADDITIONAL INCOME NEEDED (subtract B from A) $ 6,955

D. AMOUNT OF MONEY TO MAKE UP SHORTAGE (at an assumed rate of interest)

  6%—multiply by 6
  8%—multiply by 8
  10%—multiply by 10

  $ 6,955 × 10 $ 69,550

E. ADDITIONAL CASH REQUIREMENTS

  Final Expenses $ 7,500

  Education for Children 0

  Liabilities (including Mortgage) $ 37,005 $ 44,505

F. INSURANCE NEEDS (D plus E) $ 114,055

Health insurance

In recent years, medical costs have skyrocketed. Few people really know how much medical coverage they have or are entitled to, or how to file claims. They are staggered by the bills that come with a major illness.

It is essential to understand the various types of coverage, especially if you are covered by a group plan at your place of work. You should then pick out what is best for you and your family. Cost may be a major consideration, but you should get the best available for the amount you can afford to pay.

The purpose of health insurance is to protect you from high medical costs, including hospital bills, physicians' fees, and drugs. The types of coverage include:

1. *Basic hospitalization.* This is provided by private insurance companies and the various Blue Cross policies nationwide. The policy usually pays all or part of a person's hospital bills, including semiprivate room, food, X-rays, laboratory tests, operating room fees, and drugs. Usually the coverage is limited to a specific number of days during any one period, with a waiting period between confinements. The better the coverage, the greater the cost.

2. *Basic surgical and medical expense.* Again, private companies provide these policies, while the nationwide Blue Shield (usually associated with Blue Cross) is best known. Fees for doctors, whether surgeons or other physicians, are paid separately from hospital fees. Usually the insurance company sets a "schedule" of certain fees which it is willing to pay for certain operations. If your surgeon charges more than that fee, you must pay the difference. Obviously, again, the better the insurance coverage, the higher the cost.

Note: Often, basic hospitalization is combined with basic medical-surgical coverage, as in the Blue Cross/Blue Shield plans. Everyone should have at least this basic coverage.

3. *Major medical.* This type of policy starts where basic hospitalization and basic medical/surgical insurance leave off. It covers the big expenses that are above the maximums of those policies. Usually a major medical policy covers extensive hospitaliza-

tion, surgery, other doctors' fees, private-duty nursing, home medical care, diagnostic work, therapies, medical devices, and rehabilitation. Major medical policies contain a deductible feature, so the patient pays a certain amount—usually from $100 to $1,000—before the insurance company pays anything. (Often, the deductible is annual: With each new year, you pay the first $100 or so of claims yourself before the insurance company pays anything.) Once you have gone beyond the deductible amount, most major medical policies pay 80 to 85 percent of each claim you file. You must pay the balance yourself. At a still higher level, however, the insurance company takes over and pays 100 percent of all legitimate claims (this is called a "stop-loss limit"). Some policies put no limit on the maximum amount of claims they will pay. Others are limited to $250,000 or $500,000. Most policies have a lifetime maximum.

Example: Suppose you have a major medical plan with an annual deductible of $100 and a stop-loss limit of $2,000. If you have a $1,800 claim, you will have to pay $440 out of your own pocket:

Total claim	$1,800
Less deductible	− 100
	$1,700
Insurance co. pays 80 percent	− 1,360
You pay 20%	$ 340
Plus deductible	+ 100
Total you pay	$ 440

Co-insurance is the amount of the bill you pay above the deductible, with the insurance company picking up the rest, up to the policy limits. Once you have gone beyond the deductible amount, most major medical policies pay 80 to 85 percent of each claim you file. You must pay the balance yourself. Thus, you may pay 20% in co-insurance up to $2,000 or so, after which the insurance company takes over and pays 100 percent of all legitimate claims (this is called a "stop-loss limit"). Some policies put no limit on the maximum amount of claims they will pay. Others are limited to $250,000 or $500,000. Most policies have a lifetime maximum.

Once your out-of-pocket expenses (i.e., the deductible and co-insurance amounts) reach $2,000, the insurance company will pay 100%. Thus, if your benefit period is one year, you will be responsible for $2,000 each year.

How can you cut down on the cost of a major medical policy?

1. Increase the deductible.
2. Ask for a higher stop-loss limit.

Either step will mean that you increase the risk that you are willing to take. You have to decide how much risk you can shoulder. Many people would rather pay a higher premium and not have to worry that out-of-pocket expenses will send them to the bank to borrow money if a major illness occurs.

4. *Medicare*. This covers everyone age 65 or older who pays Social Security taxes or is eligible for Social Security or Railroad Retirement benefits. It is also available to those under 65 who are disabled or who have chronic kidney disease.

Medicare is divided into two parts. Part A is free of charge. It pays for hospital stays, and care in a skilled nursing home as part of after-hospital care. Part B covers physicians' fees and out-patient services at a hospital, as well as certain medical services and supplies. It costs a small monthly fee, and pays for 80 percent of "reasonable" medical costs (which often means that it pays considerably less than the actual cost). Part B does not pay for eyeglasses, dentistry, drugs, private nursing, custodial nursing home care, treatment in a foreign country, or routine physical examinations.

Clearly, out-of-pocket medical expenses can be high for senior citizens. It is imperative that they carry some supplemental policy in addition to Medicare, in order to pay for items not covered by Medicare and for expenses that go beyond the Medicare program.

Warning: A retirement nest egg can be wiped out by medical costs not covered by Medicare. Anyone over 65 must carefully consider buying additional coverage.

5. *Health maintenance organizations*. While they offer prepayment plans which provide medical protection, HMO's do not provide health insurance as such.

HMO's are organized as non-profit cooperatives. For a fixed price per month they provide medical care for their members, based on the premise that it is cheaper to prevent illness than to cure it. Since the premiums of members constitute their only source of income, HMO's must hold down costs and preventive medicine is one way to do so.

The groups own and operate hospitals and clinics, and hire doctors, nurses, and medical technicians. They pay annual salaries to their professional staffs, so the doctors do not charge patient by patient in the normal way.

If you belong to an HMO, your premium covers nearly all medical expenses and you are entitled to care in one place 24 hours a day, seven days a week. One disadvantage, though, is that usually you cannot choose your own doctor; you must use a doctor who belongs to the HMO.

Before making a decision about HMO's, find out how near the service is to you, and talk with some of its members.

Some things to look for in health insurance

• Combination plans. Many companies, as well as Blue Cross/Blue Shield, offer plans which combine basic hospitalization and medical and surgical benefits with a major medical plan. This package deal often has lower deductibles.

• Items not covered. Check on such items as cosmetic surgery, eyeglassses and routine examinations for glasses, regular physicals, and psychiatric care (if covered, the latter is usually under a special limitation).

• Guaranteed renewable and non-cancellable policies. Some companies reserve the right to cancel at any time. This could be disastrous if, when they cancel, you are uninsurable or have an illness that existed before they canceled. A non-cancellable policy cannot be canceled during the period of time it is stated to run. Nor can premiums be increased during this period. Usually when the stated period has ended, and it may be as short as one year, the policy has to be renewed if the policyholder chooses. However, the company may increase the premium.

• Shop around and consider the alternatives. Everyone should have major medical insurance. A major illness or accident can bring on economic chaos. If you are eligible for group medical insurance, take advantage of it. If not, compare the cost of Blue Cross/Blue Shield with other plans. Note the various features of each. Consider taking a larger deductible in order to pay a smaller premium. See if an HMO is near you: Often an HMO offers group coverage to an individual who is not otherwise eligible to be in a group medical plan.

Disability insurance

What happens if you are disabled by an accident or an illness? The odds of being disabled for an extended period before you reach 65 are greater than the odds of dying before then. If you are disabled, chances are high that your income will drop and your medical bills will climb simultaneously. Not only would that be no fun, it would be disastrous. So whether you are male or female, if you are the breadwinner you must have disability insurance that insures a monthly income. Use Worksheet XIV to calculate what eligibility insurance you need.

Social Security provides disability insurance for those who become severely disabled before they reach 65, but it is limited. It covers those who have a physical or mental condition so severe it prevents them from working and which is expected to last, or has lasted, for at least 12 months, or which is expected to result in death. You have to wait five months after your disability begins before Social Security starts to pay. The amount it pays is the same as the amount you would start to get upon your retirement at age 65. To be eligible, you must be fully insured under the Social Security regulations.

Disability insurance as a fringe benefit

Many employers provide some sort of disability insurance, using either of these two types of plan:

1. *Short-term.* This provides modest benefits for a short period. It usually pays weekly, based on your earnings, but with a maximum that is as low as $150 a week. The waiting period before it starts to pay is from seven to 21 days. Some plans pay out for as few as 13 weeks, while others may continue to pay up to 52 weeks.

2. *Long-term.* This is designed to take care of more serious disabilities. Most plans provide a certain percentage of earnings, usually 50 or 60 percent of your base salary, with the maximum monthly payment varying from $1,500 to $2,000 or above. The waiting period may be anywhere from three to six months. The payments may continue any number

of years (five, ten or 20) or until you reach 65. If all this sounds like a wide variety of benefits and conditions, it's because there are almost as many different disability policies as there are employers, so you have to check out what your company is offering and hope it is one of the better long-range plans.

In case you are wondering why everything seems to stop at age 65, it's because that is when Social Security and Medicare take over. Since these two government programs are so universal, and since most people have traditionally retired at 65, the insurance companies just don't bother to work out actuarial tables or develop premium rates for employee group insurance after 65. However, any number of insurance companies do offer individual policies. Many advertise that they pay a certain flat amount daily, "from the first day of hospitalization," unrelated to any medical bills or hospital costs. Such policies are carried by many people who are over 65. They are, in effect, simple disability policies.

MARTY MID'S DISABILITY PLAN . . .

It covers 60 percent of his salary, up to a maximum of $2,000 a month. If he has to call upon it, it starts payments after a six month waiting period and pays until age 65. Since his base salary is $44,000 or $3,666.00 per month, he could receive up to $2,200 per month (60 percent of his $3,666.00 or $2,200 per month). This comes in below the $2,500 maximum his group policy is willing to pay. (See page 111)

Coordination of benefits

There is one more wrinkle. In many disability policies you will find a "coordination of benefits" provision. This prescribes how other disability income benefits payable to the disabled person will affect the benefits of the group plan. If worker's compensation, Social Security, or any other policies are paying, the group policy may not pay as much as it otherwise would on a long-term plan.

Your group disability policy terminates, of course, if you leave your job for any reason, and when you reach 65.

Worksheet XIV: Example One
Mr. Mid
HOW MUCH DISABILITY INSURANCE?

A. ANNUAL FAMILY EXPENSES (Budget form) $ 45,701

B. SOURCES OF INCOME

- Spouse's Income _____ $ 9,000
- Social Security Benefits (if eligible) _____ $10,416
- Disability Benefits from Work _____ $ 26,400

Income from Income-Producing Assets
(Assets Evaluation form) _____ $ 1,550

- Other Income _____

TOTAL SOURCES OF INCOME $ 47,366

C. ADDITIONAL INCOME NEEDED
(Subtract B from A)   _____

D. AMOUNT OF MONEY TO MAKE UP SHORTAGE
(at an assumed rate of interest)

   6% multiply line C by 6
   8% multiply line C by 8
  10% multiply line C by 10   _____

Importance of individual policy

Since Social Security and group plans do not usually pay as much as you really need if you are disabled, individual policies are important. Your disability policy premium will be based on your age, condition of health, and income. Since policies can vary widely, be sure you know what you are buying.

Features that affect your coverage include:

• Maximum benefit period. The length of time during which the company will pay. Usually expressed in weeks, months, or years. Some policies run for a lifetime.

Perils insured against: either accident only or accident and illness. Be sure you get coverage for both. Some companies loudly advertise their bargain rates but cover accident only, something you don't realize until you read the policy carefully.

• Elimination period. This is the time that must elapse before the company starts to pay. It is usually 30, 60, 90, or 120 days after your disability begins.

• Definition of disability. The conditions under which you will be considered disabled for the purpose of collecting benefits.

In buying any disability policy, make sure:

1. The insurance company cannot cancel, raise the premium, or alter benefits during the life of the policy.
2. The policy is guaranteed renewable.
3. The period covered makes sense. It may be as short as one year, or continue until you reach age 65, or cover your lifetime. The longer the coverage, the higher the premium.
4. You know when benefits start. The longer the elimination period before payments start, the lower the premium.

How to know how much disability insurance you can afford—and need

Again, go back to your worksheets, especially Budget

and Asset Evaluation. Review what it costs you to live and what sources of income you would have if you were disabled. Look over your current expenses, and take into account the fact that expenses will more than likely rise if you are disabled. If you run into special medical provisions and care, they will go up like a rocket. Also consider the effect of inflation on your purchasing power.

WHAT IF JIM YOUNG DIED, OR WAS DISABLED? . . .

The Youngs' annual living expenses are now $25,860. If Jim Young were disbled, or if he died, where would this money come from? Would Dolly need just as much?

If Jim were disabled, expenses would probably increase, due to medical costs. If he died, they would decrease very little, for his child would be growing up with continuing needs such as food, clothing, and education.

If Jim were disabled, Dolly's salary and their Social Security payments would leave her just enough income to meet existing expenses. Jim should consider an insurance policy that would give extra protection.

If Jim died, Dolly's source of income, in addition to her salary and Social Security payments, would be Jim's group life insurance policy from his job. While Dolly would need additional income, she would face several expenses: 1) cash for Jim's funeral and other final expenses, 2) education for their child, and 3) clearing up the debt they are carrying. These expenses would amount to about $41,854. (See page 113)

To cover this, the Youngs should consider a one-year renewable term policy for at least $75,000. They should review it as Jim's salary and financial responsibilities increase, and also when they buy a house, and when another child is born. The premiums must come from the amount they expect to cut from clothing and entertainment expenses.

Worksheet XIV: Example Two
Mr. Young
HOW MUCH DISABILITY INSURANCE?

A. ANNUAL FAMILY EXPENSES (Budget form) — $25,860

B. SOURCES OF INCOME
- Spouse's Income — $7,500
- Social Security Benefits (if eligible) — $14,952
- Disability Benefits from Work — 0

Income from Income-Producing Assets
(Assets Evaluation form) — 0

- Other Income — 0

TOTAL SOURCES OF INCOME — $22,452

C. ADDITIONAL INCOME NEEDED
(Subtract B from A) — $3,408

D. AMOUNT OF MONEY TO MAKE UP SHORTAGE
(at an assumed rate of interest)

6% multiply line C by 6
8% multiply line C by 8
10% multiply line C by 10 — $34,080

Worksheet XIII: Example Three
Mr. Young
HOW MUCH LIFE INSURANCE?

A. ANNUAL FAMILY LIVING COSTS (from Budget form) $25,860

B. SOURCES OF INCOME AVAILABLE
- Spouse's Income $7,500
- Social Security Benefits $12,480
- Income from Income-Producing Assets (from Budget form)   0
- Income from Proceeds of Existing Life Insurance Policies (use an assumed rate of interest)

  6%—multiply amount of insurance by .06
  8%—multiply amount of insurance by .08
  10%—multiply amount of insurance by .10

     30,000   × .10 = $3,000

- Other Sources of Income   0

TOTAL SOURCES OF INCOME $22,980

C. ADDITIONAL INCOME NEEDED (subtract B from A) $2,880

D. AMOUNT OF MONEY TO MAKE UP SHORTAGE (at an assumed rate of interest)

  6%—multiply by 6
  8%—multiply by 8
  10%—multiply by 10

     $2,880   × 10 $28,800

E. ADDITIONAL CASH REQUIREMENTS
Final Expenses $5,000
Education for Children $30,000
Liabilities (including Mortgage) $6,854 $41,854

F. INSURANCE NEEDS (D plus E) $70,654

Worksheet XIII: Yours
HOW MUCH LIFE INSURANCE?

A. ANNUAL FAMILY LIVING COSTS (from Budget form) _____

B. SOURCES OF INCOME AVAILABLE

●Spouse's Income _____

●Social Security Benefits _____

●Income from Income-Producing
Assets (from Budget form) _____

●Income from Proceeds of Existing Life Insurance Policies
(use an assumed rate of interest)

  6%—multiply amount of insurance by .06
  8%—multiply amount of insurance by .08
  10%—multiply amount of insurance by .10

  _____ × .10 = _____

●Other Sources of Income _____

TOTAL SOURCES OF INCOME _____

C. ADDITIONAL INCOME NEEDED (subtract B from A) _____

D. AMOUNT OF MONEY TO MAKE UP SHORTAGE
(at an assumed rate of interest)

  6%—multiply by 6
  8%—multiply by 8
  10%—multiply by 10

  _____ × 10 _____

E. ADDITIONAL CASH REQUIREMENTS

Final Expenses _____

Education for Children _____

Liabilities (including Mortgage) _____ _____

F. INSURANCE NEEDS (D plus E) _____

Worksheet XIV: Yours
HOW MUCH DISABILITY INSURANCE?

A. ANNUAL FAMILY EXPENSES (Budget form)　　　　　　　　_____

B. SOURCES OF INCOME

　● Spouse's Income _____

　● Social Security Benefits (if eligible) _____

　● Disability Benefits from Work _____

　Income from Income-Producing Assets
　(Assets Evaluation form) _____

　● Other Income _____

　TOTAL SOURCES OF INCOME　　　　　　　　　　_____

C. ADDITIONAL INCOME NEEDED
　(Subtract B from A)　　　　　　　　　　　　　　_____

D. AMOUNT OF MONEY TO MAKE UP SHORTAGE
　(at an assumed rate of interest)

　　6% multiply line C by 6
　　8% multiply line C by 8
　　10% multiply line C by 10　　　　　　　　　　_____

Property and casualty insurance

If you had a severe fire in your home, or a hurricane or flood roared through your town, or thieves took your television and stereo and silver and priceless antiques, could you make repairs and buy replacements out of your financial assets? Few of us could. That's why property and casualty insurance is imperative.

Most of us understand the basic idea of the coverage: If a fire or theft, flood or wind damage occurs, we will be reimbursed for the loss. But few of us really understand what will be covered by the insurance company and what we must take care of ourselves.

Homeowner's policies, as they are called, usually cover:

1. Fire insurance on the house.
2. Extended coverage for damage to the house by such things as wind, hail, falling objects, smoke, and motor vehicles.
3. Allowance for additional living expenses if the homeowner has to live in a motel or rented house while repairs are made.
4. Allowance for personal property lost because of fire, theft, or mysterious disappearance. This covers items such as clothing, books, cameras, stereos, and household furnishings.
5. Liability. This covers claims based on any injuries suffered by others and caused by your property. Classic example: The mailman is bitten by your dog or slips on the ice on your sidewalk. The coverage includes payments for medical expenses.

Some key points about homeowner's insurance:

• The policy always specifies an address and provides protection at that address. However, most policies also cover losses while possessions are in storage or at the cleaner's or when you are traveling.

Items stolen from your children while at camp or away at school may be covered. Look closely at what the policy says about college dorms; most policies do not stretch all the way to a dormitory or, even less likely, to an apartment near a college campus. If your student son or daughter is living off campus in a rented apartment, better get insurance on the stereo, the camera, the walk-around headset, the guitar.

• Most policies limit the amount they will pay to the actual cash value of the property stolen or destroyed. The insurance company takes the age of the article into account and depreciates for each year you have owned it. (This is another area where your records come in handy, for if the suit lost in the dry cleaner's fire was new only six months ago you will have a way to prove it.) Since actual cash value may be substantially lower than what it will cost you to replace an item, especially considering the way property has appreciated in recent years, this insurance policy can be costly to you. However, you can get a replacement endorsement added to your policy by paying a higher premium. If a major loss occurs, you will consider the money well spent.

• The typical standard homeowner's policy limits the amount the company will pay for a loss of personal property. Usually the limit is 50 percent of the total amount that the building is insured for. The loss is also limited to that caused by a fire, windstorm, or other specific peril listed in the policy. If you have a valuable collection of art, jewelry, silver, antique furniture, or other similar objects, you will be wise to ask for a "personal property floater schedule." It broadens the policy's coverage, but it can be expensive. By having appraisals made, the company gives a cash value to each item you list on the schedule. If you add this coverage, remember to re-evaluate these items at least every couple of years, as the value of collectibles rises with inflation. (The trend can go the other way, too, of course: Remember what happened to the price of silver between 1979 and 1981? It shot up dramatically, then fell right back.) Also update the schedule to delete any items you no longer possess. Usually this type of coverage has a deductible amount, to help keep down the premium cost.

Important: Your record-keeping, including inventory of items, receipts for purchases, and photographs, is vital if you are carrying a personal property floater on your homeowner's policy.

• Homeowners are not the only ones who need coverage. If you are renting, you need both personal property and liability coverage just as much as if you were the owner. A person who falls and is injured can sue the tenant as well as the landlord.

What about the amount of insurance you should carry on your home? This mainly depends on the replacement value of the house and its contents. With inflation and its resulting appreciation of homes over recent years, you cannot just let your homeowner's policy sit year after year without updating it. In fact, most of the insurance companies and their agents add an increment yearly for that upward spiral and simply bill you for the increase. The question, really, is whether that automatic increase is enough. Have you brought collectibles into the house? Do you need appraisals of certain valuables so you can take out a personal property floater? Since the floater is relatively expensive, do you want to insure only those items that would be really difficult to replace, such as heirlooms? Are you keeping smaller items in a safe deposit box and handling the risk that way? All these are questions that you should consider—and act upon.

Speaking of suing

You should be aware that while liability insurance covers you against a claim by a person bitten by your dog or injured on your icy sidewalk, it does *not* cover you in a situation where a repairman, cleaning woman, gardener, or painter is injured while working in your home. They should be covered by worker's compensation. Never just assume that a repairman or housepainter or other contractor has his or her own insurance, though. Ask to see proof.

How much liability insurance should you carry? Usually the range is between $25,000 and $300,000. With the number of liability claims and the size of the settlements in our society today, it is not a bad idea to increase your coverage to as high as $1 million if you have a fairly substantial income and assets. People who are suing are usually advised by their lawyers to try for as much as they can and to dig the well where the water is.

Automobile insurance

This is required by law in most states, and if you drive one inch without it you are courting financial disaster.

There are four things to understand about auto insurance:

1. *Liability coverage.* This protects you, the owner of the car, from claims that may result from the injury or death of another person, as well as

from damage to property. The other person may be a pedestrian or a passenger or driver of another vehicle. The situation itself may be of any kind; the newspapers regularly report crazy happenings involving vehicles that no one could have anticipated. The property may be another vehicle or any kind of stationary object.

The liability part of the policy is written in figures that look like this: $100,000/$300,000–$25,000. What does it mean? The first two figures mean that the insurance company will pay up to $100,000 for bodily injuries to any one person and up to $300,000 for injuries to two or more persons in any one accident. The $25,000 means they will pay that maximum for property damage.

SUPPOSE MARTY MID IS CARRYING $100,000/$300,000–$25,000 . . .

In an accident he hits a Rolls Royce containing four people; their injuries add up to medical claims of $400,000. If he cannot defend his situation and loses a lawsuit, he will be personally responsible for $100,000 of medical claims and for the difference between $25,000 and the replacement cost of the Rolls Royce. Far fetched? No! Read your newspaper.

---

2. *Collision.* This pays for damage to your car caused by a collision with another vehicle, or with any other object, whether it is stationary or moving. To cut down the premium cost it carries a deductible, usually $100 or more, so you pay for minor repairs yourself. Usually the company pays for the cost of repairs above the deductible amount or pays the actual cash value of the car, less the deductibility, if you total the car. When buying a policy, you can usually choose how much of a deductible you want to risk. The higher the deductible, the lower your premium, of course.

3. *Comprehensive.* Many things, in addition to other vehicles, can damage your car. This part of the insurance covers loss due to fire, theft, wind, hail, and falling objects. Again, a deductibility clause may reduce your premium.

4. *Medical payments.* All passengers injured while in your car are covered by this section. It also covers the members of your family while they are riding in any other vehicle.

When you are buying auto insurance, or reviewing what you have, be aware of these important points:

• Like all other insurance, policies need to be reviewed and updated regularly. Nothing stays the same.
• Premium rates vary according to where you live, and according to the amount of risk you are willing to handle yourself by taking higher deductibility. Rates in big cities are higher than in small towns and rural areas, presumably because the heavier the traffic, the more likely an accident.
• Unless you simply cannot afford it, your liability coverage should be the maximum possible. If you have substantial assets, you should have substantial liability coverage.
• As your car gets older, its value depreciates. Watch its cash value. If you keep a car several years, there comes a point when you may consider dropping collision coverage altogether because the annual premiums approach the replacement value of the car.

• Shop around. Auto insurance is high-priced stuff, but there are many insurance companies competing for your business. Your best approach is to work with an independent agent to get the best coverage for the lowest premium.

Summary

Whether you are considering or reviewing life, health, disability, property and casualty, or automobile insurance, ask yourself these basic questions:

What if? What if this, what if that? What risks do I take? What things could possibly happen?

Which of these risks must I assume myself, and which can I pay an insurance company to take over? That, in turn, will determine what kinds of policies and coverage you need.

How much will it cost? Shop around. Get several quotes, or bids, from various agents and companies. Make your decision based on coverage, service, and cost.

From time to time ask yourself this question: Am I carrying enough insurance, or too much, for my situation right now? Reevaluating and updating your policies every so often is most important.

KEEPING FIT AFTER 65: RETIREMENT

11

"Will my health decline?"
"Will I lose my marbles?"
"What about my self-esteem, with no job to go to?"
"What will I do with my time?"
"Will I have enough to live on?"

The problems facing the person who is retiring are psychological, medical, social and economic. Many of the economic problems result from failure to plan for the time when work will no longer structure your day or define who you are and how you feel about yourself. Up to this point your job has given you a sense of belonging, as well as being a way of providing for your family. It has given you a sense of worth and of accomplishment.

Now, for many a retiree, there comes a sense of emptiness and loss of identity. In numerous cases—though fewer and fewer each year—the wife has not had an outside job and the sudden continual presence of her husband makes her feel her domain is

being invaded. The very fact that he is on hand for lunch every day, a meal she may not have had to cope with for 35 or 40 years, may mean completely altering her schedule. A period of adjustment, that may well involve an identity crisis at age 65 or so, is very likely inescapable.

More serious problems may stem from worry about money matters. Income during retirement generally comes from Social Security, pensions, and individual savings and investments, areas that may be hard hit by inflation. As Florida Representative Claude Pepper, chairman of the Select Committee on Aging of the U.S. House of Representatives, said in a hearing on September 17, 1980:

> The current retirement income system has not kept its promise to the workers who faithfully paid into the Social Security [system], placed their faith in private pension plans, and tried to frugally invest in savings accounts during their working lives. Inflation has ravaged their retire-

ment savings or made it impossible to save, while their pension expectations have vanished into an incomprehensible maze of requirements or often disappeared because of the requirements that a worker participate in a plan for ten years before he becomes entitled to pension benefits . . . We must come to grips with the failure of pension plans and savings plans to play their intended role in contributing to retirement income security.

This is the Broken Promise of Retirement. It has made retirees dependent on others. It has shattered their dreams and created despair and want.

Few people stop to think that inflation is selective. It does not hit everyone in the same corner of the pocketbook, nor with equal severity. Its effects vary depending on where you live and on what products you buy and in what proportions. Those living in rent-stabilized apartments in large cities with good public transportation systems do not feel the impact of oil prices, for instance, in the same way as people living in rural or suburban areas who are dependent on cars and on oil for heating their own homes.

The elderly are probably the hardest hit. Their incomes usually stay essentially the same, no matter what inflation does. As inflation has zoomed skyward, it has left them with less and less to spend on non-necessities. As incomes barely cover food, shelter, medical care and transportation, inflation has reduced the standard of living of many retired people.

What will your needs be after you retire?

Fares to and from work, business lunches, work clothes—all these expenses will be cut out. The kids' educations will be paid for; chances are the mortgage will be, too. That leaves three key areas to think about:

• Emergency fund. Even if you haven't needed one all these years, it's a good idea to set up a fund for special emergencies.

• Lifestyle. It is time to rethink your priorities. Will the two of you still need two cars? Will travel become a larger budget item than before? Will you be entertaining more or less often? Some budget

items will shrink, others stretch as your retirement lifestyle evolves.

• Budget. If you have kept a regular budget in force, you have a good fix on where the money goes now. Look over the various categories and see what they may cost in the future, assuming there is no change in lifestyle. Usually a retired couple can live on 75 percent of their pre-retirement gross income. This means you will have about the same net income as before retirement. The reason? Deductions from your gross income will decrease. You will no longer be paying into Social Security, unless you continue to work on a part-time basis, and your taxes will be less because Social Security benefits are not taxable, and also because those over 65 may take an extra exemption on their federal income tax returns. Thus if a married couple are both over 65, they will have $3800 in personal exemptions plus the standard deductions amount of $5,600 allowed by the government for married couples. As a result, income up to $9,400 will not be taxed.

You will need about the same spendable income to maintain your present pre-retirement lifestyle. While certain expenses will be reduced or become nonexistent, others, such as medical care, will increase. And, of course, we cannot forget about inflation.

Analyzing assets in retirement

Your Asset Evaluation Worksheets (Chapter 9 on Evaluating Assets) really prove their worth when you contemplate retirement. They sum up your acquisitions over the past 35 or 40 years—and raise many questions. They help you to look closely at each and every asset and think objectively about it. Should your assets, whether income-producing or non-income-producing, be exchanged for something that would produce additional income or benefit you in some other way?

People of retirement age do not easily change their way of thinking about money matters. After 30 or 40 years of investing in "safe" institutions such as passbook savings, they are not about to go into money market funds. Resisting change is easy. "I've been doing it this way for 35 years" . . . "I don't like it" . . . "It won't work—I know" . . . "It's too late to make changes now" . . . "It's not practical."

Just the opposite is true: It is highly practical to take hard-earned dollars out of a low-income-producing account and let them earn more for you. In fact, it is imperative.

The means for creating a better lifestyle—for you, not for your heirs—is probably right under your nose. Look at your assets. What alternatives do they offer? Can you get those that are already producing income to produce *more*? Do you keep too much cash in a checking account that pays no interest? Move it into a savings account, then transfer money to checking only when you really need to.

Have you got too much in a low-interest-yielding savings account? Buy a certificate of deposit or move it into a money market fund that will produce more income. Find the highest interest rates that are paid without tying up the money for extremely long periods (you should keep it reasonably available in case you need it).

Look at the stocks and bonds you bought some years back. Are they low-income investments? Do you have low-interest bonds sitting around? Countless people do. Often a safe deposit box reveals mature Series E bonds that have been forgotten. Some people think they shouldn't sell a stock because "we bought it so cheaply years ago and if we sell we have to pay taxes on it."

Having to pay taxes should never be a deterrent to selling. The fact is, you pay a *capital gains tax* on any stock held for over a year, but you pay only on 40 percent of the gain you made.

WHAT HAPPENS WHEN THE ELDERS TAKE A GOOD HARD LOOK AT ASSETS . . .

Once he had accumulated money in savings, Frank Elder made his first stock purchase: 50 shares of Sears Roebuck in 1956. He got a 2-1 split in 1977. A 100-share purchase of U.S. Steel was split 3-2 in 1972, giving him 150 shares. In 1969, Frank bought 15 shares of Standard Oil of New Jersey (which later became Exxon). There were 2-1 splits in 1971, in 1976, and again in 1981.

These stocks add up to a current value of $21,665 with income of $928—46% of which comes from Exxon. The total yield is 4.2 percent. (See below) The Elders have $5,000 in a certificate of deposit adding $425 in income at 8.5 percent. Thus their average yield on interest and dividend income is 4.9 percent, obviously too low. Let's look at the Elders' Asset Evaluation Worksheet on page 122.

RECORD-KEEPING (Segment of Worksheet IV)
Mr. and Mrs. Elder

3. SECURITIES
Stocks & Mutual Funds:

Number of Shares	Company	Date Purchased	Cost
100	Sears	1/16/56	$1,769
150	U.S. Steel	2/27/63	$4,700
100	Westinghouse	8/29/63	$3,650
300	American Motors	11/18/65	$2,625
120	Exxon	7/15/69	$1,084

Current Market Value	Owned By	Location of Stock Certificate	Annual Income
$4,100	Mr. Elder	safe deposit	$176.00
$3,375	Mr. Elder	safe deposit	$180.00
$5,400	Mr. Elder	safe deposit	$140.00
$750	Mr. Elder	safe deposit	0
$8,040	Mr. Elder	safe deposit	$432.00

TOTAL $21,665   TOTAL $928

Worksheet XII: Example One
Mr. & Mrs. Elder
ASSETS EVALUATION

INCOME-PRODUCING ASSETS Current Assets	NET SALE VALUE	ANNUAL INCOME (From Budget)	% YIELD (Income ÷ Market Value)	ANNUAL COST OF OWNERSHIP (From Budget)
Checking Accounts	$500	0	0	
Savings Accounts				
Credit Union Accounts				
Money Market Funds	$5,000	$425	8.5%	
Certificates of Deposit				
Treasury Bills				
Treasury Notes				
Securities				
Stocks	$21,665	$928	4.2%	
Bonds				
Mutual Funds				
Total	$27,165	$1,353	4.9%	
NON-INCOME-PRODUCING				
Personal Residence	$28,000			$2,880
Recreational Property				
Cash Value Life Insurance				
Business Interests				
Home Furnishings	$10,000			
Automobiles	$2,000			
Jewelry	$10,000			$1,800
Antiques—Fine Art				
Coin Collection				
Stamp Collection				
Total	$50,000			$4,680

YOUR PERSONAL FINANCIAL FITNESS PROGRAM

The first thing the Elders should do is sell the four stocks which are not producing the income that Frank and Gertrude need. These stocks have not increased in value as Frank had thought they would. The Elders should maintain the $5,000 in the certificate of deposit for emergencies. The $13,625 that they will receive from the sale of Sears, U.S. Steel, Westinghouse and American Motors should be invested. At various rates of interest, it can produce:

- at 8%, $1090 or $162 more
- at 10%, $1362 or $434 more

How should they invest the $13,625? They should consider certificates of deposit, government backed securities, bonds (which can be bought at a discount and will produce steady income), or stocks with high yields.

At some point, the Elders will have to consider selling some of the jewelry that Frank has given Gertrude over the years. If and when they do, they must be sure to get several appraisals and deal only with reputable people. It will be important for them to study the market for such items before they sell; they may find that it isn't worth it.

Other assets must be examined. Perhaps they should sell the retirement home they bought. With the proceeds from investing its equity, they could pay rent and be better off. Maintenance expenses would be less, too. If they could live near public transportation, they could cut out a big expense: the automobile, with its upkeep and insurance.

Getting more income from assets

Let's look at some ways that you can make assets produce more income.

We'll start with stocks. Say you have stocks that originally cost $10,000. You sell them now for $25,000. The gain is $15,000. You will have to pay a tax on the gain.

Suppose these stocks have been yielding 5 percent annually. The income would be $1,250. By selling the stocks you could have $21,570 available to reinvest, assuming you are paying tax at the 23 percent rate. If you put it into investments paying 10

percent, your income would be $2,157 or $907 more than you were getting before.

You may also have a loss that can give you an advantage. Many people in the 1950s and 1960s bought long-term corporate bonds which yield 5 percent. As interest rates have soared in recent years, such bonds have become worth less and less: You may even own a bond that is actually worth less on the open market than when you bought it. You can thus take a loss by selling such corporate bonds.

Suppose you bought a corporate bond for $10,000 and it is now worth only $7,500 on the market. That is a loss of $2,500. You can apply that loss to your $15,000 gain from the sale of stocks, reducing your total gain to $12,500. Paying taxes should not be a deterrent to selling stocks and bonds.

What about assets that are not producing income? What are your choices with them? Is there a way to invest for more income? How can you turn an asset that costs a lot to own into an asset that produces income? Check out the following and please don't close your eyes and say, "No, I won't sell that," until you've read it.

1. *Your home.* The house is probably your largest investment, yet it also carries heavy expenses—fuel, taxes, insurance, upkeep. Are they getting you down? Have you had it with the crabgrass? Have you let the new roof you need go by the board because it is too expensive? Do you and your mate rattle around inside the house? When you get right down to it, is too much of your money tied up in this non-income-producing asset?

Look around in your area at the alternatives that might be suitable. Depending on where you live, you might:

- Sell the house and invest in another, smaller house. You would have some money left over to invest in other ways. Or, if the new cost were about the same as the old, you would still gain because upkeep on the new, smaller house would be less.

- Sell and try a mobile home if you live in an area where they are suitable and popular.

- Sell and invest the money; use the income to pay rent.

Suppose you sell the house for $80,000 and buy a small condominium for $50,000. If you invest the remaining $30,000 at 10 percent, it will produce

$3,000 in additional yearly income. You might start saving on expenses if the condo costs less to maintain. Or you might invest the entire $80,000 at 10 percent, producing an income of $8,000 a year, which can pay rent of $667 per month. If you rent for less, more income can be produced.

A caution on selling your house. Remember that there will be selling expenses: real estate commission, closing fees, moving expenses (which are high), such miscellaneous expenses as carpeting or drapes in the new place, and unforeseen expenses. Don't let any of these surprise you.

Another warning: If you are thinking about a major geographic move, give the place a trial at its worst time of the year. If you think Florida or the sun-belt Southwest is the place to spend your retirement, basking in hot February sunshine while those back home shiver and shake in the cold, go down there in July and see how you make out in 110 degrees. Some like it fine. Some find out too late that they should have stayed where they were.

There's another aspect to the retirement move, too. You'll want to have airfare to visit children and grandchildren. You might think right now that they will come to you, but it is doubtful that they will come frequently enough to satisfy your longing to see them, and the expense might be more than they can handle at this stage in their lives.

2. *Recreational property.* The cottage at the lake or shore, the ski hut in New England or northern Michigan—are you using it as much as you once did? With the children off in other areas, pursuing other interests, is it a justifiable expense? Chances are it is difficult to rent (and if you do rent it, you must manage its maintenance by remote control, which is no fun) and you are paying insurance and property taxes and getting little out of it.

If that sounds like *your* "second home," it is time to sell it and reinvest the proceeds to produce income.

3. *Cash value life insurance.* Do you really need the insurance? Is it paid up, or are you still writing checks for premiums? Every policy has a table of guaranteed values. For instance, for a $10,000 policy purchased at age 35, the following are some of the options available at age 65:

a) Cancel the policy. Say you have a $10,000 policy in force. The cash surrender value is $5,504,

so if you surrender it now your wife would lose $4,496 if she were widowed. But if you surrender it you will save $230 annually on the premium. You will invest the $5,504 at 10 percent, producing $504 a year, and with the premium saving of $230 that will give you $734 per year you do not have now.

b) Borrow on the policy. Say you borrow the full amount of cash value: $5,504. This would leave $4,496 of insurance in force. However, you must still pay the $230 premium, and you will have to pay interest to borrow the $5,504, probably $275 a year. So between paying the premium and paying the interest, your income from the investment would be reduced to $229—surely an expensive way to keep $4,496 of insurance in force.

c) Take out a reduced paid-up policy. The $10,000 might provide about $7,860 in paid-up insurance. You would still have insurance, but it would be a smaller policy. Your only saving is the $230 annual premium.

d) Use cash value to buy a term policy. The table of guaranteed values will tell you the length of the term in years, months, and days. For instance, $10,000 of cash value at age 65 might buy 16 years and 147 days of term coverage. If you should live longer than that, the policy would be finished and you would be on your own with no coverage.

e) Purchase an annuity. Your policy probably also tells how large an annuity you may buy for each $1,000 of cash value. If an annuity is what you want, shop around for the best deal. You do not have to buy it from your present insurance company; nothing prohibits you from cashing in the policy and taking the money elsewhere if you can get more per $1,000.

4. *Collectibles.* Fine art, silver and gold, books, musical instruments, antique autos, rare coins and stamps, antique furniture—you name it, none produces income. All of them require care and insurance, though. Some also need polishing regularly.

Are your collectibles still giving you the satisfaction they once did? Are you holding onto them "for the children"? Are some of them locked away in vaults or safe deposit boxes because our robbery-prone society makes them vulnerable at home?

In a word, are you trapped by possessions?

The younger generation often says: Pare down. Some younger people have no interest in polishing silver or maintaining antiques. If you are holding onto collectibles for your children's sake, the best thing to do is talk it over with them frankly. Find out if they are really interested in something that has sentimental but not intrinsic value. You may be in for a surprise.

Then, after you have discussed it with them, remember that only *you* can decide between the possible income that could be derived from selling your collectibles and investing the money, and the sentimental value of holding onto them.

If you decide to sell, get appraisals. Do your homework. Silver and gold, of course, are not priced as high as they were a few years ago, but don't let that stop you. (In fact, during the "silver rush" many people accepted the silver content value but failed to get the antique value on items they sold; in their greed over high silver prices, they actually got less than they should have.)

The question of holding things for the children brings up the larger question of what you leave for your heirs.

Who says, Never invade principal?

As you go into retirement, it is important to remember that *you are responsible for yourself*—for your own interests. There is no reason to feel guilty about how much you are leaving or not leaving to children and grandchildren. What is important now is to maintain your purchasing power in the face of inflation's power to eat away at the value of the dollar.

Many who are currently at retirement age grew up in the school that says it is all right to live off income from investments but the principal should never be touched. Preservation of capital, that's the most important thing, they say. But isn't the quality of life you are living just as important as the preservation of capital? What is wrong with using a certain percentage of your capital every year? If you used 3 percent a year, it would take you 33 years to use up a given amount of capital even if the remaining balance were not earning interest over the years.

You should find out your life expectancy from the insurance charts. For the average man of 68, it is 12 years. Suppose you doubled that to 24 years and decided to use a certain percentage of capital each year for 24 years? To many, such thinking is heresy. Yet such changed thinking could help prevent inflation's bite on your retirement income and could improve your basic standard of living.

What is important is to realize that only you know your needs. Do the paperwork. Talk to advisers and make your needs known to them. Be frank with sons and daughters. And, when necessary, shed guilt—as well as gilt.

THE ELDERS' BROKEN PROMISE . . .

The Broken Promise of Retirement. It *was* a promise to the Elders. Society promised them that if they saved and invested, they would be able to retire in comfort and with a standard of living they were accustomed to.

The Mids have had no such promise. They have seen what has happened to their parents and know that during the working years still ahead they must plan to help themselves—something that their parents never felt they had to do. In addition to Social Security and a pension plan, they must have another plan.

IRA: individual retirement account

Before 1982, only workers who had no pension or profit-sharing plan at their place of work were eligible to establish IRA's. From 1982 through 1986, anyone who had earned income could contribute to an IRA, building a nest egg while at the same time paying less federal income tax. Starting in January 1987, the rules regarding contributions to an IRA were drastically changed.

Here's how it works:

When you put money into an IRA, you may deduct it from *gross* income (that is, income before taxes). In effect, you reduce your taxable income because the interest you earn, as well as dividends and capital appreciation, are not taxed until you take the money out of the IRA in your retirement years. At that time, presumably, your tax bracket will be lower because you will be earning less.

How much may you put in each year? If neither husband nor wife is covered by an employer pension plan, they may take the full $2,000 per worker or $2,250 per one-income-couple deduction—regardless of income. For those with adjusted gross incomes between $25,000 and $35,000 on a single return or between $40,000 and $50,000 on a joint return, the maximum $2,000 deduction will drop—in steps. There will be a loss of $200 of the IRA deduction for each $1,000 of additional income. For example, if the adjusted gross income on a joint return is $42,500, a deduction of $1,500 may be taken; the deduction drops to $1,000 if the adjusted gross income is $45,000 and to $500 if the adjusted gross is $47,500. The deduction is completely phased out for the individual taxpayer with an adjusted gross over $35,000 and for joint filers with over $50,000. If one spouse does not work, the other may contribute to an account in the name of the non-working spouse. The account will belong to the non-worker. In this case, the total that may be contributed to both accounts is $2,250 or 100 percent of the compensation of the working spouse, whichever is less. The couple may divide the contributions between their accounts as they choose, but no more than $2,000 may be contributed to the account of either one.

Control of the funds in either account is in the hands of the spouse in whose name the account is held. Should a divorce occur, a partner who gets alimony and has no earned income may use the alimony to continue the IRA contributions, up to $2,000 annually. However, those who may not take the deduction may nevertheless continue to make non-deductible contributions up to $2,000. Earnings on the accounts will not be taxed until the funds are withdrawn. For those who are unable to deduct contributions, there will be no income tax on the contribution when withdrawn at retirement. Taxes will be due, however, on the earnings.

Do you have to put the maximum into the IRA each year? No. You may put as much as you want to or feel you can afford. You can make a single deposit of your entire amount for the year or put it in in dribs and drabs. Amounts may vary from deposit to deposit and from year to year, and if necessary you may skip one or more years. An IRA may be opened and first deposit made as late as the due date of your income tax return, usually April 15 of the year following.

What about getting the money out of an IRA? It may be withdrawn any time after age 59½ without penalty. Before that, withdrawals incur a penalty, except in the case of disability or death of the account holder.

Nobody says you *have* to take the money out at age 59½. But you must begin to withdraw the money by the time you are 70½ or face some stiff penalties. You may also continue to make deposits until you are 70½ but no later.

How is the money paid out to you? Again, you have choices.

1. You may take the entire sum in one lump payment.
2. You may decide to receive it in regular installments over a fixed period of time. This period may not be greater than your life expectancy or the averaged combined life expectancy of you and your spouse.
3. You may choose an annuity that will make regular payments for as long as you or your spouse live.

What about taxes on the money you put in the IRA? When you start to make withdrawals, the money you take out is taxed as ordinary income. That means of course, that if you take it all out in one lump sum, you will be taxed in that year for the entire amount.

What if you withdraw the money before you reach 59½? It will be taxed as ordinary income. A penalty of 10 percent will also be charged on the amount you withdraw. For example, if you take out $2,000 before you are 59½, you will pay tax on that amount and also pay a $200 penalty.

What happens to the money when you die? A surviving spouse who inherits an IRA account upon the death of his or her spouse, may make a tax-free rollover to an IRA.

Must you always keep the money in the same IRA account? No. You may move it to another account, in another bank, if you wish, either by direct transfer or by "roll-over." In a direct transfer, you never gain possession of the money during the transfer. It is moved directly from one trustee to another. For example, you may ask your bank to transfer the funds directly to a mutual fund. In a roll-over, on the other hand, you actually get a check or cash out of the bank. You must then deposit it in another IRA account within 60 days or pay tax on it as ordinary income and pay the 10 percent penalty.

Note: After any roll-over, you must wait at least 12 months before you may take another; direct transfers are not limited to any waiting period.

Does it make any difference when you make your contributions? It sure does. If you deposit money in an IRA early in the year, in January, say, that money and the interest it immediately starts to earn are tax deferred—protected from any tax for that year. And your money has that much more time to grow. If you put the money into a regular savings account or money market fund, to wait until you move it into an IRA before the April 15 deadline the following year, the interest it earns will be taxable.

IF THE YOUNGS START AN IRA . . .

Suppose Mr. and Mrs. Young start an IRA with $1,000 a year but wait until the end of the year to make the contribution. They have friends who put the same amount in at the beginning of the year. Each account earns 10 percent. At age 65, the Youngs will have about $442,592 in their account. Their friends will have about $486,852—or $44,260 more than the Youngs.

Does an IRA really make a difference?

Yes. If you put in the maximum of $2,000 a year for 10 years and it earns 10 percent, you will have about $35,062 in the account at the end of 10 years. If you put the same amount, at the same interest, in an account where you pay taxes on it, you will have about $23,000 in 10 years (assuming you are in the 25 percent tax bracket).

Does it make any difference where you invest the funds?

Yes. Plenty of banks, insurance companies, brokerage firms, and mutual funds are clamoring for your money. IRA funds can go into almost any type of account. So you need to look at all aspects of your situation and make a decision. How long do you plan to make contributions? What type of risk are

you willing to take? If you are now in your 50's you may want to select an investment with a guaranteed yield. If you are much younger you may be willing to take a risk, knowing that if there are losses you will have time to make up the difference. How much are you willing to contribute each year? Some IRA's allow you to make small or frequent contributions. Others do not. Following are descriptions of some of the ways you can set up an IRA. Before deciding on anyone, you should get specific information from the institution you are considering.

1. *Banks.* Most offer a variety of options patterned on the conventional certificate of deposit. Options involve the kind of interest, the amount of interest, and the length of time of the certificate. Some offer variable or floating interest; others do not, so you should compare interest rates offered by different institutions. In most, you can open the account with as little as $100.

2. *Credit unions.* Most credit unions design their IRA's to fit the size and nature of the union. The rate of interest is set by the board of directors. Your initial deposit may be quite low, and deposits may be deducted directly from your paycheck if your employer is willing to extend such a benefit. This means real convenience for you.

3. *Insurance companies.* An IRA set up with an insurance company is an annuity. A minimum rate of interest will be fixed through the years, possibly high in the early years, then lower as time goes on. You may have to pay an annual fee and sales costs, with a sizeable penalty if you withdraw the money prematurely (probably even higher if you withdraw in the early years of the policy).

4. *Mutual funds.* In this case you buy shares in a pool of money that is invested in securities chosen by professional money managers. In some mutual funds, your IRA is in a money market fund, where the investment is in short-term securities and the rate of return varies daily. In others, the investment is in stocks and bonds, some in blue chip companies, others in more risky emerging companies. As your investment objectives change, you may move your IRA from one mutual fund to another. In order to do this, many people choose a company that operates several funds. Most funds

require a minimum deposit, some as low as $100. Usually a yearly maintenance fee of $2 to $10 is charged.

TIPS ON IRA'S

• Shop around. Financial institutions are in competition—for your money.

• Check for payroll deduction plans. Your employer can make it easy to build your retirement needs. Weigh the safety of various investment options.

• Compare minimum amounts required to open IRA accounts.

• Understand the kind of interest or other return that is offered. It makes a difference in the dollars coming to you. Interest on $1,000 contributed every year at 8 percent will give you about $49,000 in 20 years. At 10 percent, you will have about $63,000.

• Compare interest rates. They vary from locality to locality and from institution to institution. And they can change during the lifetime of your IRA, so keep an eye on them over the years in case it becomes wise to make a direct transfer or a roll-over.

• Keep an eye on the marketplace, too. Continue to study the options available so you can make informed decisions on transfers or roll-overs.

• Don't wait. Start an IRA as soon as you can. While you do not have to contribute every year, you should get into the habit. And remember—while the 1986 tax laws have reduced the value of the IRA as a tax deduction, the fact that earnings are not taxable until funds are withdrawn makes the IRA a very attractive way to save.

---

5. *Investment brokers.* These offer the widest range of IRA's. You can build your own portfolio, using a "self-directed" plan. You make the decisions on investing in stocks, bonds, mutual funds, unit investment trusts, or limited real estate partnerships. Each time you buy or sell, you pay commissions. There are also administrative fees. Most brokers expect you to invest the entire $2,000 at one time and it is really best to accumulate $10,000 to $15,000 before you start to self-direct.

Remember: Investing in securities carries the risk of loss as well as gain, but it is the most flexible IRA route you can choose.

To summarize: It is never too soon to start an IRA. The commitment is long-term, but well worth it, especially in view of current widespread concern over the future of Social Security, pension plans, and inflation.

IF THE MIDS START AN IRA . . .

Since their adjusted gross income is above $50,000 they will not be able to deduct their $4,000 in IRA contributions. They want to save for retirement and know they will benefit on the long-term tax-deferred feature of the IRA. Let's say they each put in $2,000 for 14 years. They will each have contributed $28,000 and each account will contain nearly $50,000, assuming an 8 percent interest rate. This fulfills half of the Mids' goal of accumulating $200,000 in 14 years. (See Chapter 2 on Goals.)

The Mids have seen what happened to the Elders. They have decided to start cutting back on expenses and are developing a specific retirement plan. They are aware that at an inflation rate of 8 percent, a 1981 dollar will be worth 29 cents when Marty Mid retires in 2001. The Mids know that they must seek investments that will appreciate in the years before retirement. Once they are finished with college bills, Marty plans to start a payroll deduction plan at work, having his company deduct about $250 each month. This will fulfill the other half of the Mids' retirement goal.

The Mids have talked about inflation and tried to grapple with it. They figure it is here to stay and must be part of their financial planning. From their letters and phone chats with the Elders, they have seen how it can hit retired people, especially since many of their expenses, such as food, transportation, medical costs, and utilities are not inflation proof. They have sensed the anger and frustration of the Elders as their expenses rise and their retirement income stays the same.

Because they want to know how vulnerable they will be, the Mids are figuring out their own inflation index. Here's how they do it: Taking their total budget figure, they subtract the education figure. This gives them $30,950 annually. They then consider all current expenditures in the budget to see which are not inflationary, such as mortgage payments, loan repayments or IRA contributions that do not change with time. The total affected by inflation comes to $21,465. They divide $21,465 by $30,950 to get an inflation index of 6.9 percent.

This formula, which is more accurate than government figures, means that they must keep their income and savings growing by at least 6.9 percent to keep abreast of inflation.

For the self-employed: Keogh plan

Any self-employed person should consider starting a Keogh plan as a nest egg for retirement. In all respects,

Keogh has the same rules and regulations as an IRA, with one important exception: You may contribute as much as $30,000, or 20 percent of income (whichever is less) each year.

The IRA and the Keogh plan are bonuses given by the government. They may be the most important keys to maintaining your lifestyle during retirement. They can help to mend the Broken Promise of Retirement, but only if you make the effort to learn about them, analyze your own needs, ask questions, understand the options, and be aware of changes in Social Security and pensions law.

EIGHT BASIC STEPS TO MONEY MANAGEMENT IN RETIREMENT

1. *Determine probable retirement income.* How much will you get from:
   Social Security
   Pension plan
   IRA and/or Keogh plan
   Current investments
   Interest on savings
   Veterans and disability benefits
   Dividends on life insurance policies in force

2. *Determine probable retirement expenses.* What will be the costs of:
   Relocating (one-time expense)
   Rent, mortgage, household maintenance
   Food
   Medical (including insurance)
   Transportation (local)
   Entertainment
   Travel (distance)
   Miscellaneous

3. *Evaluate assets.* Look at other resources that can make a difference:
   Home
   Collectibles
   Cash value of insurance

4. *Diversify investments.*
   Get rid of deadwood.
   Know your needs and invest in what will be right for you.
   Do not put all your eggs in one basket.

5. *Consider income-producing employment.* Under 1982 Social Security regulations you could earn up to $6,000 without penalty. In 1983, if you are over 70, there is no limitation.

6. *Learn to economize.* Shop thriftily.

7. *Evaluate insurance needs.* Chances are that policies bought some years ago no longer meet your changing needs. See Chapter 10 on Insurance.

8. *Involve your spouse.* You and your spouse should each know how your money is earned and spent. And each of you should know how to manage if the other is disabled, whom to contact for advice, and where all your important papers are kept.

FINANCIAL FITNESS FOR WOMEN ON THEIR OWN 12

"What household bills do I need to pay now?"
"Maybe I should sell the house right away . . ."
"Am I still covered under his medical insurance?"
"Why didn't we ever talk about these things?"

The average widow in this country is 56 years old. She is destined to spend 20 years on her own. Eighty percent of all women will live alone at some point in their lives.

Despite these surprising statistics (more like staggering, if you suddenly find that you are one of them), most women have not been involved in family finances. They have handled household money and everyday expenses, yes, but few have a solid grasp of insurance matters, taxes, or pensions, or know the whereabouts of valuable papers or loan agreements. Traditionally women have felt, and been encouraged to feel, that someone will take care of them, make all the decisions, and see that everything turns out all right.

It seldom happens that way. All too frequently, after a divorce or the death of a spouse, a woman finds herself not only in emotional turmoil but faced with sudden and confusing financial responsibilities. Well-meaning friends and family give her advice and, willy-nilly, she often follows.

In fact, just the opposite should happen. Since, on average, women outlive men, they should learn financial responsibility early on—not only the mechanics of paying bills, but how to handle all the decisions that affect their financial security. Many of the decisions made before a woman is living alone will affect her afterward, yet when a husband says, "Sign here, dear," and offers a contract, tax return, or other financial obligation, many a wife obligingly takes pen in hand and never thinks to read or query the document.

Signing anything without bothering to read it is a mistake. When you get a chance to look over an income tax return, study it; you can learn a great deal about your own financial situation. When you sign a contract or agreement, read it thoroughly, for once you have signed it you will be just as liable as your husband for its consequences.

Blame English common law—and Blackstone

How did the system ever get this way? It began with English common law, on which our legal system is based, and with Blackstone, who codified common law. He said, "Husband and wife are one . . . that one is the husband."

Before the Industrial Revolution, women were an integral part of what is now called "cottage industry." The home was the factory. But all money that was earned was turned over to the husband—it belonged to him. A century or so ago, an early female physician who was owed payments for her services had to have her husband go to court to get the money because legally it belonged to him.

With the Industrial Revolution, the family changed from a unit of production to a unit of consumption. The work place moved out of the home, leaving most wives behind. A husband who could not support wife and family was considered a failure and only poor and immigrant wives took jobs (at extremely low wages, by the way) to support the family.

The leisured class of women needed to worry about little outside the household. Because financial transactions were considered too complicated for women to manage, husbands arranged for others to take control of their money when they died, on behalf of their wives. Even though money and property came to be in their names, women were usually relieved of the duties and responsibilities of financial transactions.

In fact, it was only as recently as January 1, 1980, that Louisiana husbands were stripped of their status as "head and master" of the household. Up until then, a husband could sell the house or the car, borrow money, or make just about any financial deal without his wife's permission and with money that was, in truth, his wife's as much as his.

The disillusionment of divorce

Chances are that a divorced woman will have to get used to downward mobility, for it is almost impossible for two separate parts of a family to maintain the lifestyle they had when they were one family.

If you have taken financial security for granted, never knew what your husband's income was, never handled any finances more complicated than the grocery money and maybe the regular monthly bills, readjustment can be rough. For the first time, you may be confronted with a limited fixed income from alimony or child support and with responsibility for the security of your children and yourself.

As a divorced woman, you must set goals and priorities that are realistic for you and your family. You must budget carefully. If you are returning to work but have young children, you must arrange for child care. If you are working, your employer may provide reasonably good medical coverage through a group plan; if you are not working, you will need your own medical plan.

Use this book to plan your financial situation as a single person. Be realistic about your goals and spending, and look beyond today. Remember that every investment decision is *your* decision.

A widow faces countless questions

The widow who best handles her inheritance is the one who has been involved in family financial matters all along, doing more than just writing checks and handling the household budget. But such financially fit women are in the minority.

Most widows are confronted not only with grief but with financial matters of which they know very little. Questions arise daily: How do I start Social Security payments coming? Where is the key to the safe deposit box? Which bills should I pay now? Should I take the lump-sum payment the insurance company is offering? Should I sell the house right away? How does his pension plan work—and do I get benefits under it? What about medical insurance?

If you are newly widowed, make no financial decisions for at least six months to a year. It takes that long to determine what your needs are going to be. Meantime, hold on to your inheritance. Later, when things settle down, make educated decisions.

How can a woman become financially fit?

Clearly, it is essential for a woman to learn how she

will handle money if and when she lives alone. The key to learning is open communication between spouses. However, if a husband has had total control of the finances and is unwilling to let go of the power, this can be a problem.

Here are some important points a couple should discuss and steps they should take.

1. Talk about how the woman will survive if the husband dies.

2. Be sure the wife knows where all important papers are kept.

3. Make a point of having the wife meet the husband's financial advisers and get to know them. (She may ultimately find that they are not the ones she wants to keep, but they should be consulted by a widow before she makes any major decisions.)

4. The wife should open her own checking account. If she is working, her earnings can go into that account and she can take responsibility for certain agreed-upon expenditures. If she is a homemaker, and not working, her husband should give her a certain amount each payday for groceries and other household expenses. The budget worksheets in this book can help determine the right amount. (With her own checkbook and responsibilities, a woman learns what money can and cannot do and, if she manages well, what is left over is hers to blow. As long as there is food on the table and bills are paid, no woman should have to report to anyone or account for where the money is going.)

5. The wife should also establish her own credit history. This can be difficult, sometimes almost impossible, to do after a divorce or the death of a husband.

6. The wife should also get into the habit of reading the financial pages of the newspaper and the monthly financial magazines.

7. The husband and wife together should attend some classes on financial planning.

8. Both should get involved and older children should be included, too.

Finances should be a family matter.

IF MRS. MID OR MRS. ELDER ARE WIDOWED . . .

Gertrude Elder would lose her Social Security payment each month, but would continue to collect her late husband's. She would receive $15,000 from his life insurance policy, and would choose to take it in a lump sum so it could be invested. Each month, she would have:

- His Social Security $714
- Income from invest-   77
  ments they made
  before he died
- Income from $15,000
  life insurance invested
  at 10 percent   125

        Total $916   (or $179 less
                               than the
                               Elders' retire-
                               ment income
                               before he died)

Except for taking the lump sum life insurance payment, Gertrude Elder should wait at least six months to a year before making any decisions. During this time, she should consider whether to realign her investments for a higher yield. She might also think about whether to live nearer to town. As one widow said, "If and when I move, I've got to be near public transportation. As I get older, I might not be able to drive."

WHAT IF MARTY MID DIES? . . .

From Mr. Mid's How Much Life Insurance Worksheet on pages 106 and 107, we know that if Mary Mid is widowed, she will have available income of a little over $28,000. If Marty buys additional insurance of $100,000 to cover final expenses and all liabilities except education, she will have this amount to produce additional income.

Mary should not use the insurance money to pay off the mortgage. Her monthly payments are small, the interest is deductible on her income tax return, and is only 8 percent—low enough to hold onto these days. She can make more by investing the insurance money. (Of course, many people purchase mortgage insurance through the bank or other lending institution that provided the mortgage, naming them as beneficiary; such insurance pays off the mortgage whether you like it or not.)

When she reaches 65, Mary will start receiving 100 percent of Marty's Social Security benefits. If she elects to start benefits between the ages of 60 and 65, the amount of each check will be less. The checks at 65 will be higher than the amount she is earning on a part-time basis.

Mary may decide to go into full-time work until she is 65. But she should consider this over a period of six months or more. If she works full-time she may be covered by a pension plan, depending on what her employer provides, and she will gain such benefits as medical and, perhaps, dental insurance. She will need to study her options and make her own choices. With $125,000 of insurance coming to her, she will have to consider whether to take one of the options the company offers or accept the lump sum and invest it. Wisely invested, her $125,000 could make a big difference not only now but during her own retirement years.

The key point is that she must learn the options—by getting involved—before she comes to a decision. And she must not let anyone rush her.

Women must take on their own financial management. They must seek out information and training, broaden their horizons and take responsibility for their actions, so they are ready if and when they have to live alone. Chances are great that most women will have to live alone at some time during their adult lives.

It could happen to you.

LET'S FACE IT, WHAT WILL YOU LEAVE BEHIND?

13

YOUR WILL

"Should my wife have a will?"
"Just what is 'Probate,' anyway?"
"Estate planning? That's for rich people, isn't it?"
"How can I be sure people will get what I want them to get?"

The purpose of a will is to make certain that your property goes where you want it to go after you die. It is your means of making decisions, putting them on paper, and seeing to it that the paper becomes a legal document that no one can argue with.

If you die without a will, you will be said to have died "intestate." In that case, the state in which you lived immediately before death becomes responsible for deciding who gets your property. Its decisions may or may not fit the ideas you had, but only those left behind will know that. Most likely, it will not agree with what you had thought should be done, for the possibilities of inequities are great.

Just as this book has been created to give you control over your money, your will gives you control over not only who gets what, but how and when. It conserves and distributes your estate the way you want it done. It names guardians for any minor children you leave behind. (Nothing is worse than a family squabble over who is to take care of children; often a split occurs, with elderly grandparents taking charge and with the children enduring still another turnaround when the grandparents die.)

"Estate" is another of those bugaboo words. It simply means everything you own: your money, your house and land, all your worldly possessions. Estate planning is planning for what becomes of it all. It is really nothing more than caring for those who will survive you. If you have followed this book's instructions, you are well on your way to estate planning already, because:

- You have your papers and records in order.
- You know your assets and who owns what.
- You understand income and expenses.

- You know how much life insurance you have—and need.
- You know about your Social Security benefits and pension benefits.

Your will should be reviewed regularly, at least every five years. Here are some of the reasons a will may need to be updated:

- the birth of a child
- the death of a beneficiary or of the executor (the person you have chosen to handle the details of the will when you die)
- marriage or divorce
- a move to a different state, where the laws may be different
- a major change in your financial circumstances
- new laws affecting estates.

Do women need wills?

Yes. Women have property of their own. If nothing else, they usually have personal property, such as jewelry and heirlooms, that they want to pass on to a child or a grandchild. In addition, they usually inherit property from their husbands.

If a woman does not have her own will at the time when her husband dies, she should immediately make one. Obviously this is a difficult chore just after the death of a husband, though. It is much better to make a will when your husband makes his, and then to make changes, as needed, six months or more after his death.

There is another important aspect to a wife's will: It should name the same guardians for the children as the husband's will names. This will avoid a custody fight if husband and wife die at the same time.

Consult a lawyer

Even if you think you don't have enough worldly goods to justify making a will, take a look around you. Insurance policies, company benefits, your home, investments, household furnishings—all may add up to more of an estate than you may have thought you had.

You should have an attorney draw up your will. A good lawyer will know your state's laws, and will avoid problems that you might create by making your own homemade will. To save his or her time, and your money:

- Have ready a list of your assets (from your Net Worth Statement).
- Choose an executor, a friend or relative whom you trust. This person will be fully responsible for seeing your will through probate and making sure your estate is disposed of. This person should live nearby. If he or she dies, you must revise your will to name another.
- Choose a guardian for minor children. Guardians must provide proper care as well as manage money for the children.
  Caution: Do not get into the embarrassing or awkward position of naming a guardian without first approaching the candidate on the subject.
- Decide how you want your estate distributed (that is, who gets what).

Finally, ask your attorney to keep the original signed copies of your will, and your spouse's, in his safe. Keep copies in your files at home.

Another dreaded word: Probate

Your estate is either of two types: *probate* and/or *taxable*. If an asset is jointly owned and does not go through the probate process, it may nevertheless be part of the taxable estate. Since federal estate and gift tax laws frequently change, and since state laws vary greatly, you should ask your lawyer to discuss and explain what happens to a taxable estate where you live.

The function of probate court is to authorize and supervise the payment of funeral expenses, taxes, and debts owed by the person who dies, and to authorize the cost of administering the estate (usually your executor is paid for handling your estate). The court then sees that any remaining property is distributed to the beneficiaries or to those who are entitled to it.

The executor works under the court's supervision and scrutiny. If you do not have a will, the court — acting for the state — will name an administrator.

The probate procedure includes:

1. Probating the will. Application is made for

probate of the will, which is filed with the court and declared valid. The court approves the executor named in the will, or names an administrator.

2. Posting of a bond by the executor or administrator (unless your will waives the requirement). The amount of the bond will depend on the size of the estate.

3. Inventory of all assets that are owned in your name *alone*. This is needed to determine whether your estate is solvent. Assets must be evaluated. Appraisers will be called in to judge the value of real estate and certain collectibles such as coins, jewelry, and so on. An up-to-date Net Worth Statement can be a great aid at this point.

4. Advertising for claims against the estate. This is in case any unknown debts are "out there" somewhere. The notice will specify that all claims must be submitted within a stated period of time, otherwise they need not be honored. At the same time all recent and outstanding bills, such as funeral or medical expenses, are paid.

5. Filing of state and federal tax forms, as required by various laws, and payment of the taxes.

6. Final accounting and distribution of the remaining estate to those named in the will.

That, in simple terms, is the probate procedure. It involves certain time limits set by state law (the inventory, for example, must be completed within a certain time). The entire procedure can take anywhere from nine months to two or three years, depending on the complexity of the will, size of the estate, and number of beneficiaries.

Note: Once a will has been probated, it is a matter of public record. For this reason, many people prefer to establish trusts; they are not made public.

What about jointly held property?

Any property that is jointly held is not included in the probate procedure. While jointly held property used to entail decided disadvantages, the Economic Recovery Tax Act of 1981 changed the law so that for federal estate tax purposes it does not make much difference today whether or not property is jointly held. A spouse may leave the surviving spouse an unlimited amount of property without its being taxed. It will be taxed only when the surviving spouse dies, but as the taxable amount decreases each year, fewer and fewer people are being affected.

State inheritance tax laws are different. No two states seem to be alike. Many have neglected to make changes that coincide with the federal law.

Jointly held property has certain advantages, including:

• It passes immediately to the survivor, staying out of probate.
• It is easy to set up.
• It assures an inheritance for a spouse with no funds of his or her own, because jointly held property cannot be sold without the permission of the other spouse.
• It can eliminate ancillary probate (that is, probate in another state). This is important, for instance, if you have a vacation home in another state. Be sure the place is jointly held, in order to avoid probate fees.
• Creditors may not be able to seize jointly held property, unless the surviving spouse assumed liability. Again, each state has different laws.

There are some disadvantages to jointly held property, too:
• Signatures of both spouses are needed in order to sell property. This can be a problem in a divorce situation or if one is absent and has not given a power of attorney to the other.
• Either spouse can clean out a joint bank account.
• Property cannot be willed. Neither spouse has any say in how the surviving spouse will dispose of property.
• It may be subject to gift taxes.
• In a large estate, when one spouse dies, jointly held property added to the surviving spouse's estate may swell it to too large a size, making it tax prone. By careful planning while both spouses are living, wills can be drawn to pass certain property directly to the children or grandchildren.
• Accounts can be frozen by banks, preventing the survivor from using the money.

YOUR OWN BALANCE SHEET

14

Reading this book and doing these exercises should have put you well along the road to financial fitness. Now it is important to maintain your fit condition.

Don't forget how difficult, overwhelming and unattainable it may have seemed when you set out. And remember, if you are now where you want to be in handling your money matters, you can stay within that framework yet indulge yourself now and then when it is necessary or seems important to do so. What's important is to watch the dollars and cents just as you would watch the calories.

Some readers may find that they must wage a continual war—winning a skirmish here, losing a tactical fight there, but always striving to keep the upper hand. If you are one of those, you may have to do the equivalent of imposing a crash diet after a period of gorging on too many desserts.

You alone

In the first chapter, I said only you can do it. This guidebook is designed to help *you* and to be adaptable to your needs. But only *you* can take charge.

It's somewhat like exercise class. The instructor can show you which exercises will flatten out the tummy—but it is your tummy—and only you can do the exercises and get the results. The same is true of your diet. You write it down, you count the calories, you make your resolutions and line up your intentions—but you must be the one who says "no" when the dessert cart comes rolling by. This book gives you the program to follow, but it can't stop you from overspending.

Staying in good shape

Once you are in good shape, you *can* stay that way. You will have learned to take charge of your financial life—without anxiety and, in fact, enjoying the occasional binge when you know things are under control. What you have now, and can maintain, is a nice freedom of choice about what you are going to do with your money.

Let's review some of the key points of your financial fitness program. Remember that the exercises may be a little different for each person, just as the exercises in a physical fitness program are a little different for each body's needs.

The following is a summary of what you need to continue doing in order to stay in shape. Don't ever forget that a diet or a physical fitness program is built step by step, one on top of another. Nobody ever ran in a marathon, at least not for very far, without at least some stretching exercises, jogging and short runs. So every phase counts toward your total fitness.

1. Did you establish your goals?

Are they realistic? You wouldn't expect to shed 10 pounds within a week after starting your physical fitness program—and you can't expect to get money matters under control in a matter of days, either. But just as it can be realistic to take off 10 pounds in a month or so without starving to death, it is also possible to reach your financial goals given sufficient time.

(Idea: You might even think about combining physical and financial goals. What if you decided to take off 10 pounds by a certain date and at the same time to save a certain amount to buy a new outfit by that date?)

2. Did you get your records in order?

Before you go on a diet, it's a good idea to clean all those fattening foods out of the kitchen cabinets. Before starting your exercise program, it's vital to have the right running shoes and/or whatever other equipment you may need. Before getting your financial house in order, it is equally important to toss those useless slips of paper into the trash and set up a sound record system that will help you keep track of where things are—and where you are.

3. Did you use the financial worksheets?

Remember, I said your initial net worth statement is the key to knowing where you stand. It's like weighing and measuring yourself before you start your physical fitness program. Where do you stand now?

Your budget is like keeping track of where your diet is going. It is the mirror that reveals *your* bulges. If there comes a moment of truth—that your pants are still too tight—then you have to decide how you can reduce further.

4. Is credit a problem?

Some people manage to maintain a binge despite their diets. "I'll buy that irresistible suit now, then lose weight. By three months from now, the suit will look great on me." But a year later the suit is still in the closet with its price tag still attached.

Have credit cards enabled you to stay on a binge? Is your budget bulging with credit payments, month in, month out, so you have little left to spend on other items? If you have decided to kick the habit and get into shape, you will have to go on a really strict diet. As outlined in the chapter on credit, you may even have to go cold turkey—like taking doctor's orders to get in shape and lose weight fast before you get into deep trouble. Heart attack, diabetes—a rough time awaits those who overextend their physical credit. Bankruptcy awaits those who overextend financial credit.

5. What about Social Security and pension plans?

This is a little like assembling the ingredients and the cookbooks that will help you make a healthy and tasty meal even though you are on a diet. Find out what you will be receiving from Social Security and your company pension plan, if there is one. Know now what your financial benefits will be. After all, you wouldn't start a physical fitness program without knowing what the expected benefits were.

6. Have you checked out your assets?

Assets vary at different stages of life. Evaluating them every so often as you go along is like keeping up with your weight control and changing physical exercise needs at different stages of life. No one follows the same program at 45 or 55 that they followed at 25. And no one's assets are the same, or have the same uses, at those different ages. Use asset evaluation as a measuring tool. Know what it is costing you to own those assets and how much income you are receiving from them at any one time.

7. *Determine insurance and retirement needs.*

Should I realign my assets to produce more income? Should I swim five more laps just to stay in the shape I'm now in? Should I establish an IRA? Good questions to ask yourself and to answer regularly.

Whatever its purpose—covering your life, your home, your medical bills or your automobile—your insurance must fit your individual needs. This is like doing specific exercises for the part of your own body that is most out of shape. Don't forget that having too little insurance could be like losing too much weight: It's unhealthy. By paying more than you need to in premiums when you can't justify the coverage can be equally bad.

Also remember that insurance needs change. Adequate coverage today may not be enough tomorrow, when your family has grown or you're earning more or the expensive college years for the kids are at hand. Assess your risks frankly. List them and add them up. Then figure out what insurance you need

in order to handle them. Whatever you do, don't be guided by what insurance your neighbor is buying, any more than you would blindly follow your neighbor's physical fitness program.

8. *Be ready to live alone.*

Your financial fitness program must help you prepare for the time when you will have to live alone for some period. So be aware that if someone else has always cooked the meals and handled your diet, you might very well go off on a binge the first time you are alone in the kitchen. Learn your financial fitness habits while you have your spouse with you. Cook them up side by side and get plenty of practice at handling them alone.

Keep this book as your reference and guide. Don't ever hesitate to go back and re-read or re-do the exercises you need most. Above all, keep control now that you are in charge. Being in charge of your money will not and must not be an activity that brings you uneasiness, worry or fear. It's just the opposite, in fact. Taking charge, making the handling of money a regular daily activity, will put you in a continuing state of sound financial fitness, which in turn will give you peace of mind.

INDEX